Postcards

An Advanced Listening and Notetaking Workbook

Susanna L. Minton

Ann Arbor

THE UNIVERSITY OF MICHIGAN PRESS

To my parents, who instilled in me a passion for travel,
education, and language

Copyright © by the University of Michigan 1998
All rights reserved
ISBN 0-472-08493-3
Published in the United States of America by
The University of Michigan Press
Manufactured in the United States of America

2001 2000 1999 1998   4 3 2 1

To the Teacher

Postcards: An Advanced Listening and Notetaking Workbook is a textbook, with accompanying audiocassette, focusing on improving lecture listening and notetaking skills of high-intermediate and advanced students who are preparing to study in English-speaking universities and others who need to listen at length in English. Each lecture in *Postcards* focuses on the history and culture of a different North American city, with interesting side trips to areas near three of the cities studied.

To facilitate students' use of the text, each chapter has many consistent features.

Pre-Listening Activities

Pre-listening activities are structured so that the students can prepare for what they will hear in the lecture. Students answer prediction questions (Predict!) often based on examination of the photographs in each chapter, explain what they already know about each city, and become familiar with vocabulary expressions (Vocabulary Preview) they will hear in each lecture.

Notetaking Strategies

Following the pre-listening activities, students will be given one strategy for taking notes in a second language. The notetaking strategies focus on such skills as identifying the main idea, distinguishing important information, learning how to anticipate what's coming in a lecture, and abbreviating notes. A notetaking outline or guide is provided in each chapter to aid students in following the lecture while taking notes. Symbols, including arrows and lines, may be indicated in some of these notetaking outlines. The symbols are meant to help students connect ideas that are related. Each notetaking strategy builds on the prior ones taught. In some chapters, a notetaking exercise is given so students can practice the new strategy before listening to the lecture. Teachers should go through each notetaking strategy with students prior to the first listening of the lecture. Students may then practice the new strategy by working through the notetaking exercise, and then move on to using the strategy while listening to each lecture twice. It is important that a teacher examine students' notes after each lecture to ensure the specified skills are accurately learned.

First and Second Listening

Students will listen once for general information in the lectures. They will be aided in their notetaking by listening guides, which help students to pick out and remember the most important information given in the recorded lectures. These guides will contain less and less information as students progress through the book. By the end of the program, students will have learned how to identify the important information in a lecture by themselves, without the help of the listening guides. For the Second Listening, students will hear the recorded lectures again and take notes on important details, listening for the more specific information.

Post-Listening Activities

The post-listening activities allow students to practice what they learned from the lectures by answering discussion questions and participating in other interactive, comprehension-based activities in which they must use their notes. Other post-listening activities include: Vocabulary Blitz, in which students reexamine the vocabulary previewed earlier in the chapter, using it in new contexts and examining word forms associated with each expression; Writing about What You've Learned invites students to associate their new knowledge of each city with information they already possess in an informative written response, using vocabulary learned from the lecture; in Read More about It, students will read an article related to the culture of the city they have learned about and answer questions based on the text. These readings offer cultural information about each city in a way that is very different from the lectures. The readings are authentic magazine or newspaper articles, some of which use regional slang and references to history learned in the lectures, and they offer unique views of each city. The Tell Us More about It activity asks students to research a subtopic related to each city studied. These subtopics come from references in the lectures, so students will have a basic familiarity with them. Students are asked to research the topic and then organize an oral or written presentation. The teacher may choose to alternate between oral and written reports from chapter to chapter, depending on the focus of the syllabus, but it is important that students have practice in doing both types of projects to improve the various language skills.

Acknowledgments

I want to thank the following people whose help was invaluable in getting this project completed:

- My colleagues at DePaul University's English Language Academy, especially James Cohen and Barth Landor, for their help in the final proofreading of the manuscript; Joe Vergara, for his computer assistance; and Linda Hillman, for her support and expertise.
- My former colleagues at Boston University's Center for English Language and Orientation Programs, especially Barbara Bliss and Pamela Couch, for reading early drafts of the chapters; Terrence O'Neil and John de Szendeffy, for their test run of the lectures early on; and Jacqueline LoConte, for her constant support and guidance.
- Steve Molinsky for his motivation and encouragement in getting this project started.
- Elizabeth McCulloch, for piloting the material with her Hungarian high school students and offering valuable feedback.
- Sarah and Barry Forward, for their research and feedback on the Vancouver chapter.
- Trine Tondering, for offering valuable feedback on the lectures from a non-native speaker's perspective.
- Mike Bell, for his Philadelphia and Colonial Williamsburg photographs.
- Alix and Michael Quan, for their wonderful photography and assistance in putting the final pieces together.
- My students, for their feedback and opinions on the *Postcards* material.
- Eric, for his constant love, support, and understanding.

Contents

1 | *Phoenix, Arizona*
"The Valley of the Sun"

Predict!
Discuss the following questions with your classmates.

1. "The Valley of the Sun" is a nickname for Phoenix. What do you think it means?
2. Look at the pictures in this chapter. What do you think are the major industries in the Phoenix area?

Vocabulary Preview
From the list that follows, choose the meaning for each of the underlined expressions. You will hear the first sentence in each pair again when you listen to the recording about Phoenix. The second sentence in each pair uses the same vocabulary in another context.

a. save
b. related to farming
c. remains of a building or another structure that has been destroyed or has decayed
d. reported information that is not necessarily true but could be
e. system that supplies farmland with water
f. large and interesting
g. handmade objects that are of archaeological interest
h. danger

____ 1a. From the ancient <u>ruins</u> of the Hohokam Native American settlement rose the city of Phoenix.

1b. When I went to Turkey, I visited the <u>ruins</u> of many ancient cities.

____ 2a. They lived in a farming society that had an advanced system of <u>irrigation.</u>

2b. Proper <u>irrigation</u> is essential for crops to grow well.

____ 3a. Tourists can still find ruins, canals, and <u>artifacts</u> of their ancient culture.

3b. Many <u>artifacts</u>, like statues and pottery, still survive from the ancient Greek civilizations.

____ 4a. Gold was <u>rumored</u> to be in areas around the settlement of Phoenix.

4b. It has been <u>rumored</u> that the president will run for reelection, but no one knows for sure.

____ 5a. Although some people seeking fortunes made the adventurous trip west, many were discouraged by <u>hazards</u> of the long trip.

5b. Gasoline can be a <u>hazard</u> if you don't keep it stored safely.

____ 6a. It was firmly established as the business, political, and <u>agricultural</u> center of the territory in the southwestern United States.

6b. A great part of the American Midwest is <u>agricultural</u> and includes such crops as wheat and corn.

____ 7a. Because Phoenix is a desert community, it has always needed to <u>conserve</u> water for its residents.

7b. Please try to <u>conserve</u> your energy before the race; I don't want you to get tired quickly.

____ 8a. Completely surrounded by a series of <u>impressive</u> mountains, Phoenix is one of the most naturally attractive cities in the country and uniquely inviting because of its desert culture.

8b. Your achievements in college have been <u>impressive</u>. Not many students can maintain such a high grade point average and still actively participate in community politics.

What Do You Want to Know?

Compose two questions you would like answered by the time you finish this chapter about Phoenix, Arizona. Your questions can refer to anything about the city. Present your questions to the class to see if anyone knows the answers.

Question 1.

Question 2.

Notetaking Strategy 1: Listen for the main idea.
When you listen to a lecture, the first thing you must do is to try and figure out what the speaker is talking about, what the important information is in the lecture, and what details are necessary for you to write down. In the following lecture about Phoenix, Arizona, try to listen only for general information about the city—the major points in its history. The guide you will use in the First Listening and Second Listening will help you to pick out the most important information.

The Main Points: First Listening

Listen to the recording once to understand only the main points.

What's the Point?
Before you listen to the lecture for the first time, read these questions so you can listen carefully for the correct answers. As you listen, mark the answers to the following multiple choice questions.

1. Phoenix was first settled by _____.
   a. Spanish explorers
   b. Native Americans
   c. the United States Army
2. Phoenix is a center for business activity in the _____ region of the United States.
   a. southeast
   b. northwest
   c. southwest
3. Phoenix is a _____ community.
   a. beach
   b. desert
   c. skiing

What Do You Remember?
Briefly discuss the following questions with a classmate.

1. Describe the original settlers of the Phoenix area.
2. Describe the typical weather in Phoenix.

Details, Details: Second Listening

Listen again to comprehend some of the details about Phoenix, Arizona.

What Was That Again?

A. Read through the notes that follow. Some of the most important information is missing. As you listen to the lecture for a second time, fill in the missing information.

Part 1

• every 500 yrs. ⇨ .... lives again ⇨ rises from

....

• Phoenix rose from .... of .... Native Ameri-

can settlement

• Until A.D. 1450 ⇨ ....

• farmed and developed advanced system of ....

• intro. .... & .... to the area

• tourists today can see .... , ... , &

....

Part 2

• .... entered area in ....

• did not stay in area, but left behind .... and

....

• mid-1850s ⇨ .... arrived from .... to

this area next to ....

• Several .... estab.

• After .... Phoenix ....

....

Part 3

• Gold was .... to be in area

• Many people made trip out west, others .... by

....

• 1865 ⇨ .... built ....

• Jack Swilling ⇨ initiated .... in

....

• used old .... to direct .... to crops

• in .... ⇨ a new town was built

- real estate lots cost ⇨ .... to ....
- settlers built elaborate ....
- in ....⇨ declared capital of AZ
- center of .... , ...,

   ....
- need to conserve .... ⇨ .... community
- Roosevelt Dam ⇨ completed .... ⇨ allowed

   ....

Part 4
- 1940s ⇨ .... allowed city to become a center for

   ....
- .... made intense heat ....

   ....
- today farmers produce ....

   ....
- Heard Museum houses ....

   ....
- Phoenix Art Museum houses ....

   ....
- Phoenix averages .... of ..../yr
- attracts .... people because it has a ....

   ....
- completely .... by a series of ....

   ....

B. Now, based on your complete notes, answer the following questions to help you better understand the details of the lecture.

    1. The city of Phoenix was named after _____.
        a. an ancient Egyptian city
        b. a bird
        c. an ancient Indian settlement

2. The Hohokam tribe of Native Americans introduced _____ into their society.
   a. a successful irrigation system
   b. successful cotton-farming techniques
   c. mysterious artifacts

3. Early Spanish explorers arrived in what is today the area of Phoenix in the early_____.
   a. 500s
   b. 1600s
   c. 700s

4. Many people traveling to the Phoenix area _____.
   a. were searching for gold
   b. were killed by Indians
   c. brought wood with them to build houses

Adobe style mission

5. The invention of _____ made Phoenix a more attractive city to live in.
   a. the airplane
   b. the automobile
   c. air conditioning

Post-listening Activities

After listening twice, you're ready to examine information included in the lecture more closely.

Discuss the Details
With a partner, discuss the answers to the following comprehension questions. Write notes from your conversation for each question. Be prepared to explain your answers to the class.

1. Discuss the culture of the Hohokam tribe of Native Americans. When did they arrive in the area that is today Phoenix? How did they survive over the years? What happened to them?
2. Why were white American settlers attracted to the area around Phoenix? Once they arrived there, what kind of lifestyle did some of them lead?
3. Why did Phoenix grow during and after World War II? What type of industries are present in the city today?

What Really Happened?
Tom is confused about his visit to Phoenix. He is getting all the facts wrong when he tells his friend Liz about the trip. Correct his errors.

The first thing I did when I got to Phoenix was to visit the ruins of the Huckamuck Indian tribe. They came to this northwestern region a long time ago but have not lived there for 200 years. They were gone by the time the Spanish came in the sixteenth century. But large numbers of people didn't begin to live in this area by the Pepper River until after the War of 1812. The next thing I did was to visit the Hoover Dam. Did you know that it was built as long ago as 1922? I'm sure glad they invented effective heating systems because the weather in Phoenix can be scorching hot. My favorite place of all in Phoenix, however, was the Harold Museum, which has a great collection of western American art. All in all, this beautiful city surrounded by lakes and valleys is the perfect vacation destination for a free and easy guy like me.

Vocabulary Blitz

Word Forms
Try to figure out the correct form for each vocabulary word in the chart that follows. (Some words don't have different forms. Those are marked with Xs.)

Noun	Verb	Adjective	Adverb
ruins			XXXXXXXXXXX
irrigation			XXXXXXXXXXX
artifact	XXXXXXXXXXX	XXXXXXXXXXX	XXXXXXXXXXX
	rumor		XXXXXXXXXXX
hazard	XXXXXXXXXXX		
	XXXXXXXXXXX	agricultural	
/	conserve		XXXXXXXXXXX
		impressive	

Note: When used as a verb, *rumor* is always used in the passive voice.

Practice with Word Forms

Now, choose the best word form for each of the following sentences.

1. She made quite an _____ on her prospective employer.
   a. impress
   b. impressive
   c. impression

2. He is studying _____.
   a. agriculture
   b. agricultural
   c. agriculturally

3. They had to _____ the land before they could plant the crop.
   a. irrigation
   b. irrigate
   c. irrigated

4. That is a _____ place.
   a. hazard
   b. hazardous
   c. hazardously

5. As a _____, he would like to see the government protect endangered animals.
   a. conservation
   b. conservationist
   c. conserve

6. I heard a _____ that you are going to quit your job.
   a. rumor
   b. rumors
   c. rumored

Vocabulary in Context

Check your definitions from the Vocabulary Preview. Fill in each blank with the appropriate word from the following list. Remember to change the form of the word when needed.

ruins	irrigation	artifact	hazard	rumor
	agricultural	conserve	impressive	

1. Because we haven't had a lot of rain lately, it is important to _____ water when cooking and bathing.

2. I heard a _____ that our school's English Department will be getting a grant of one million dollars for more classes.

3. This summer I visited the _____ at Pompeii, Italy, which were a result of the destruction caused by Mount Vesuvius in A.D. 79.

4. Be careful when you are gardening. There are many _____, like poison ivy and bumblebees!

5. From the seventeenth through early twentieth centuries, the economy of the United States was largely based on _____ products, such as corn and wheat.

6. The eruptions of the Hawaiian volcano are sometimes very _____, with large flows of lava and hot steam bursting out of the mountain.

7. Valuable _____, such as a telescope, anchor, and gold coins, were found at the sight of the fifteenth-century shipwreck.

8. Farmers in the midwestern section of the United States have developed a successful system of _____ for their crops.

Writing about What You've Learned

Describe a city that you know very well. Is this city a lot like Phoenix? Why or why not? Try to use at least four of the vocabulary words learned in this chapter in your writing.

Read More about It

Read the following news article, then do the exercises that follow it.

Hohokam Pottery Turning to Dust on Museum Shelves; Humidity Fluctuations Leave Artifacts "Vulnerable"

Arizona Republic, February 20, 1995, by Miriam Davidson

Museums are supposed to preserve treasures from ancient civilizations, not let them crumble to dust. But that's what is happening at the Arizona State Museum, which holds the world's largest collection of Hohokam decorated pottery. To curators' horror, humidity fluctuations inside the museum's storage areas have caused salts in the clay to migrate to the surface, where they **flake off**. Images of birds, snakes, lizards, geometric shapes and other designs are being reduced to piles of powder on the shelves.

flake off
fall off in tiny bits

Experts are doing what they can, but what they really need is a new building. Losing the pottery—jars, bowls and scoops that the Hohokam used in daily life, religious ceremonies and funeral rites—means losing the chance to glean valuable information about one of the Southwest's most advanced ancient cultures. "It's a problem for all museums in arid climates, but the Hohokam red-on-buff ware seems particularly vulnerable," said Jan Bell, curator of collections at the museum. "Almost all of those pieces show damage."

Members of the Pima tribe, whom most experts believe are descended from the Hohokam, and the Maricopa tribe also are concerned. The state is failing in its promise to care for the artifacts, the tribes say, and the situation adds urgency to their plan to reclaim all Hohokam materials taken from Indian land.

Officials at the University of Arizona, which administers the museum for the state, have known of the salt problem for at least a decade. They say the only permanent way to stop it is to renovate the museum, at a cost of $13 million to $15 million. "It's on our capital plan, and we'd like to get to it, but we need a state appropriation," said Mike Cusanovich, UA vice president for research. Cusanovich said the university cannot issue bonds to remodel the museum because it is technically not part of the school's academic or research functions. "We're hopeful that, with the turnaround in the economy, we can convince the Legislature of the importance of this," Cusanovich said.

The Arizona State Museum collection is housed in two brick buildings on the university campus, both of which date from the 1920s and '30s. The renovation plans call for consolidating the museum into one building with 10 to 15 climate-controlled storage rooms. The museum houses 200,000 artifacts, mostly from ancient cultures of the Southwest and Mexico, and includes 19,000 ceramic pieces excavated by archaeologists.

Curators have tried to minimize damage from wildly fluctuating humidity levels by covering windows, putting up insulation, and working with the maintenance staff to regulate the mix of inside and outside air. The museum also has purchased more than a hundred specimen cabinets to help preserve thousands of delicate items such as woolen blankets, wooden masks, musical instruments and kachina dolls. But the pottery collection is too large and fragile to put in cabinets. Curators have found that soaking some of the most severely damaged pots in distilled water stops salt from rising to the surface. However, they worry that soaking also removes food residue and other evidence about how the pots were made and used. "Although we're hesitant to do anything, it's better to treat and stabilize a vessel than to lose it entirely," conservator Nancy Odegaard said.

Most of the museum's approximately 1,000 Hohokam pieces—the largest Hohokam collection in the world—were taken from Snaketown, a village on the banks of the Gila River that was inhabited from about 300 B.C. to A.D. 1400. UA archaeologists who excavated the site in the 1930s and '60s unearthed most of what is known about Hohokam culture.

Bell said the Hohokam pottery is especially susceptible to damage because of the high salt content of both the clay and the soil in which the pottery was buried. UA archaeologists working in the 1930s inadvertently contributed to the problem by adding salt to the plaster they used to reassemble broken pots. Salt makes plaster dry faster.

Fred Ringlero, director of land-use planning and zoning on the Gila River Indian Reservation south of Phoenix, says the Snaketown collection always has belonged to the Pima and Maricopa tribes, and they plan to reclaim it within the next few years. Raymond Thompson, director of the Arizona State Museum, said that also is his understanding. "If they're able to get their facilities in order before we get ours in order, so much the better," Thompson said. "The important thing is to protect the collection." Ringlero said the tribes have funds to build a small **repository** for artifacts uncovered during Central Arizona Project construction on the reservation, and may be able to put part of the Snaketown collection there. However, in keeping with tribal members' wishes, the many sacred objects that were taken from Hohokam graves at Snaketown will be reburied.

repository
a place where something is stored

UA officials say the museum still will need a climate-controlled building, even after the Snaketown and other Native American collections are returned. "Over the next 10 years, the amount of material we're storing will decrease substantially, but it won't go down to zero," Cusanovich said.

What More Did You Learn?

Discuss the following questions, based on the previous article, with a partner. Be prepared to explain your answers to the class.

1. What is the problem discussed in this article?
2. What are they doing to solve the problem?
3. Why is it so important to save these objects?
4. Why is pottery so susceptible to the deterioration?
5. What will happen to the Hohokam artifacts?

Analyze It

In groups of three or four, analyze the problem the museum is having and create a long-term plan to solve it. You may use any part of the plan discussed in the article, but you must justify whatever you decide on with the facts of the problem. Take notes when talking with your group.

Tell Us More about It

Prepare an oral or a written report on one of the following topics. Use the outline that follows to organize your presentation and take notes.

Hohokam tribe of Native Americans	Spanish in Arizona
desert life	ranching
Roosevelt Dam	Heard Museum
western American art	air conditioning

Topic:

Major points to discuss about this topic:

1.

2.

3.

4.

Details to discuss about each major point:
Major Point 1

Major Point 2

Major Point 3

Major Point 4

2 | *Vancouver, British Columbia*
"The World within a City"

Predict!

Discuss the following questions with your classmates.

1. What do you already know about Vancouver or about Canada in general?
2. Why do you think Vancouver is called "The World within a City"?

Vocabulary Preview

From the list that follows, choose the meaning for each of the underlined expressions. You will hear these phrases again when you listen to the recording about Vancouver.

a. friendliness
b. rough and possibly dangerous
c. added to a larger part
d. easy entry

e. small pieces of wood that help start a fire
f. removed
g. collected
h. a very large number

____ 1. They mostly fished, hunted, and <u>gathered</u> food and resources there until the first European fur traders arrived in force in the 1820s.

____ 2. With the discovery of gold in the 1850s, the natives were almost permanently <u>dislodged</u>.

____ 3. The area boasted many great natural resources, but the terrain was so <u>rugged</u> that it did not attract a great number of additional settlers over the following twenty years.

____ 4. However, with ample <u>kindling</u> in its structures, the new city was ripe for the fire that consumed it in twenty minutes on June 13.

____ 5. The city had grown and <u>annexed</u> surrounding areas to the east and south, and, with the completion of the Lion's Gate Bridge in 1938, Vancouver was linked to the north, ____ allowing easier <u>accessibility</u> to the city and surrounding areas.

____ 6. Today it is home to a <u>myriad</u> of ethnic groups, with an extremely high percentage of Chinese.

____ 7. It was truly a celebration of the spirit of <u>congeniality</u> beaming from the city and its residents.

What Do You Want to Know?

Compose two questions you would like answered by the time you finish this chapter about Vancouver, British Columbia. Present your questions to the class to see if anyone knows the answers.

Question 1.

Question 2.

Notetaking Strategy 2: Dates and numbers are important.

When a lecturer gives you a date or a number, it is usually important. Listen to it carefully and make sure you write down the correct number or date. For example, *fifteen* and *fifty* sound very similar. If you're not sure what the lecturer said, don't be afraid to ask for clarification or check with another student to verify what you heard.

The Main Points: First Listening

Listen to the recording once to understand only the main points.

What's the Point?
Figure out what's most important. Here are some details of the lecture. Write down the corresponding important events as you listen once. Listen also for additional dates given by the lecturer.

about 500,000—

500 B.C.

1792

1850s

1886

—April 6

　　+25 yrs.

1890s

　　1897——

Panama Canal

1920s

Lion's Gate Bridge

WWII

Immigration

    1887

    Komagatu Maru

    Today

        Chinese

Places to visit——

    Frederick Law Olmsted

    red cedar

        place to shop and buy fresh food

        gas lamps————steam clock

mountains

climate

people

What Do You Remember?

A. From your notes, create two comprehension questions based on the main idea of the lecture on Vancouver, British Columbia.

Question 1.

Question 2.

B. Exchange questions with a classmate. Answer the questions your classmate created. Did you take enough notes to answer the questions?

Details, Details: Second Listening

Listen again to comprehend some of the details in the lecture on Vancouver, British Columbia.

A. Fill in more of the dates and details as you listen to the lecture again. Try to listen for how all the information connects.

B. After listening twice, answer the following questions.

1. Who first lived in the area that is today Vancouver?

2. What European first explored the area and when did he explore it?

3. When was gold discovered?

4. In 1897, what happened to bring more settlers through the area?

5. What was the original name for Vancouver?

6. What happened in 1914 to help Vancouver's growth?

7. Explain the Komagatu Maru incident.

8. Which ethnic group is highly influencing the city today?

9. What are some fun places to visit in Vancouver?

The Lion's Gate Bridge

Post-listening Activities

After listening twice, you're ready to examine information included in the lecture more closely.

What Happened When?

Put the following statements in chronological order by placing a number (1, 2, 3, etc.) next to each. Then, next to each statement, write the year in which the incident occurred.

__ European fur traders arrived in the area. Year _____

__ Vancouver was incorporated as a city. Year _____

__ Captain George Vancouver explores the southwestern coast of British Columbia.
Year _____

__ The Komagatu Maru incident took place. Year _____

__ Native people may have begun to live in the Vancouver area. Year _____

__ Vancouver has a population of over 100,000. Year _____

__ The Klondike gold rush occurred. Year _____

__ Vancouver became Canada's leading city. Year _____

__ The Panama Canal brought more trade to Vancouver. Year _____

__ Expo took place. Year _____

Talking about It

Lewis and Lucia visited Expo 86 and learned a lot about Vancouver. Fill in the missing pieces of their conversation about the city based on what you learned in the lecture.

Lewis: Oh, Lucia, do you remember that great park we visited during Expo 86?

Lucia:

Lewis: That's right, I loved that tree. And we had a great view of the city from that bridge. What was its name again?

Lucia:

Lewis: Oh, that's right. It was built by that family. Why was it built?

Lucia:

Lewis: Now I remember. I love history, and we learned a lot about Vancouver's at Expo, didn't we? We even learned the reason Vancouver grew so much after 1900. I bet you can't remember, Lucia.

Lucia:

Lewis: I can't believe it. You remember everything about Vancouver, Lucia. You're so smart!

Vocabulary Blitz

Word Forms

Try to figure out the correct form for each vocabulary word in the chart that follows. (Some words don't have different forms. Those are marked with Xs.)

Noun	Verb	Adjective	Adverb
	gather	XXXXXXXXXXX	XXXXXXXXXXX
XXXXXXXXXXX	dislodge		XXXXXXXXXXX
	XXXXXXXXXXX	rugged	
kindling		XXXXXXXXXXX	XXXXXXXXXXX
/	annex	XXXXXXXXXXX	XXXXXXXXXXX
accessibility			XXXXXXXXXXX
myriad	XXXXXXXXXXX	XXXXXXXXXXX	XXXXXXXXXXX
congeniality	XXXXXXXXXXX		

Now, choose the correct form for each word in parentheses in the following sentences.

1. What kind of _____ did you have last night? (gather)

2. The _____ residents of the city slept in a shelter just outside of town. (dislodge)

3. Please _____ the fire for me. (kindling)

4. When did New York _____ Staten Island? (annex)

5. How can I _____ my computer account when I'm away from home? (accessibility)

6. Wow, those people are very _____!(congeniality)

Vocabulary in Context
Check your definitions from the Vocabulary Preview. Fill in each blank with the appropriate word from the following list. Remember to change the form of the word when needed.

gather	dislodge	rugged	kindling	annex
	accessibility	myriad	congeniality	

1. The family was very impressed by the _____ of their new neighbors. The couple across the street even brought over some dinner for them on their first night in the new house.

2. I couldn't _____ the stick from the ground; it was stuck there and I had to figure out a way to remove it.

3. Dan, can you get some more _____ so this fire will burn better? There are some dry sticks in the backyard.

4. I can think of a _____ of solutions to your problem. Do you want me to list all of them or just a few?

5. We _____ flowers in the field and brought them home.

6. With this new ATM card, I can now easily _____ money from my bank account.

7. Many people in the neighborhood have tried to _____ this empty lot, but no one has been able to obtain it.

8. Be careful while you're hiking. That area is very _____, and people have gotten hurt from tripping over rocks and other obstacles.

Writing about What You've Learned

Although Vancouver may be short on history in relation to other cities of the world, it is rich in diversity. How diverse is your hometown? Write about your city's diversity. Try to use at least four of the vocabulary words learned in this chapter in your writing.

Read More about It
Read the following news article, then do the exercises that follow it.

Not China, but Close: Vancouver Is the Closest Thing to an Asian Bargain

USA Today, August 11, 1995, by Barbranda Lumpkins

Walk down Pender Street in the heart of this cosmopolitan Canadian city and you'll almost think you're in the heart of Hong Kong.

Shopkeepers hawk their wares in Cantonese and Mandarin. Crispy Peking ducks hang in the windows of butcher shops. Streets are packed with people looking for the best deals on everything from fresh seafood to beautiful silks.

This is Chinatown, five square blocks crammed with stores and restaurants, adjacent to downtown Vancouver.

It's also the place to be this summer if you're searching for an affordable "foreign" vacation without the hassle of a trans-oceanic flight.

Canada, in a word, is a bargain right now. The U.S. dollar hasn't been this strong against the Canadian dollar in nearly nine years ($ 1 U.S. equals $ 1.36 Canadian).

But why Vancouver in particular?

Listen to artist/gallery owner Yukman Lai. His reason is simple: "Vancouver is a very, very nice place."

Lai, from Hong Kong, is one of many Asians who have immigrated here in recent years—an influx that has some native Vancouverites now calling their city "Hongcouver."

For immigrants old and new, Chinatown provides a comfort zone. For vacationers, it gives a quick introduction to a new culture, new traditions.

Street signs are in English and Chinese. **Pagoda-style** phone booths and street lights decorated with golden dragons dot the avenues. An ornate archway, the gateway from the Chinese pavilion at Expo 86, to which Vancouver played host, graces the entrance to the Chinese Cultural Centre.

pagoda-style
Asian-style tower with roofs turned upward at the corners

Look up and see the recessed balconies of the older buildings on Pender Street, some dating back to 1889. Stone lions stand guard outside the cultural center, which is the pulse of the community.

"They're like our security guards to scare the evil spirits away," Yeeman Cheng, a cultural center tour guide and receptionist, says of the lions.

Security, financial and political, has always been a major draw for the Chinese here. The first wave came in 1858, the start of British Columbia's gold rush. The most recent arrivals are more apt to be people such as Lai and Cheng, from Hong Kong, fleeing the British Crown Colony before it is returned to the jurisdiction of the People's Republic of China in 1997.

Vancouver vacationers also share the sense of security.

"People (visitors) say they feel safer in our Chinatown," says Betty So, event coordinator of the Chinese Cultural Centre. "I've heard comments that we're cleaner, we're brighter."

Go ahead, feast your eyes. And your ears.

At Teck Shun Trading Co., you'll find all manner of dried things—turtle shells, lizards, sea horses, snakes, seabirds and sea cucumbers. A Chinese doctor is available to hear about your latest ills and prescribe something from the vast shelves of herbs to soothe you. Check out the ginseng, which costs $750 to $4,500 U.S. for an ounce.

"It's the best Chinese remedy there is," says Cheng, eyeing the jars holding the varieties of the herb. At that price, it better be.

Besides the herbs and spices that appear strange to most Western eyes, the other most interesting thing about Chinatown is, well, Chinese food.

Over at the Dollar Meat Store, you'll find barbecue pig, dried pig and preserved, flattened ducks that look like they've been run over by a truck in a Looney Tunes cartoon.

There's also an assortment of pig innards from which to choose. "The Chinese don't waste anything. We eat pig ears, intestines, chicken feet," Cheng says.

For lunch, stop for dim sum—an assortment of hot dumplings, stuffed buns and deep-fried pastries served from rolling carts—at one of the many restaurants. Or just settle for a huge and hearty bowl of soup that has items, some identifiable, some not, floating in steaming broth.

Want seafood? Pick the fish you want swimming in the plastic tubs outside Kam Tong and a store worker will snatch it up, bean it in the head and then filet it for you, right before your eyes. Now that's fresh.

But amid the hubbub on the streets are quiet enclaves where you can immerse yourself even further into the culture.

A calmness reigns over Dr. Sun Yat-Sen Classical Chinese Garden, named for the first provisional president of the Republic of China. The Ming Dynasty–style garden, the first of its kind built outside China, is a study in simplicity and elegance, yin and yang.

"It's quiet and peaceful," says Beverly Tempro of New York as she exits the walled gardens with her husband, James.

"It's enchanting," he adds.

As water lilies and lily pads speckle the tranquil jade-green water of the pond and koi fish soundlessly swim by, "you almost forget you're in the middle of the city," says garden manager Mary Campbell.

And in the middle of a bustling Chinatown.

What More Did You Learn?

With a partner, mark the following statements T tor true or F for false, based on what you read in the article about Vancouver. Be prepared to correct the false statements.

____ 1. Vancouver is a very expensive city.

____ 2. The gateway to Chinatown came from Expo 86.

____ 3. The first people of Chinese descent came to Vancouver in 1868.

____ 4. Today, most Chinese who live in Vancouver have come from Hong Kong.

____ 5. You can purchase all medicinal herbs very cheaply in Chinatown.

____ 6. Dim Sum is preserved, flattened duck.

____ 7. Many tourists find the Ming Dynasty–style garden in Chinatown very relaxing.

____ 8. Chinatown is a suburb of Vancouver.

Analyze It

The people of Chinese descent have neighborhoods of their own in Vancouver, so that adjustment to their new home is somewhat easier than it might otherwise be. What must it be like for a new Chinese immigrant family to come to Vancouver? Write a story of a fictional immigrant family to Vancouver. Give them a history: explain why they immigrated, how they are adjusting to Vancouver, and what their plans for the future are.

Tell Us More about It

Prepare an oral or a written report on one of the following topics. Use the outline that follows to organize your presentation and take notes while researching.

natives of Vancouver   Expo 86
Stanley Park   Gastown
Captain George Vancouver   Canadian Pacific Railroad
immigration to Vancouver   Klondike Gold Rush

Topic:

Major points to discuss about this topic:

1.

2.

3.

4.

Details to discuss about each major point:
Major Point 1

Major Point 2

Major Point 3

Major Point 4

3 | *Philadelphia, Pennsylvania*
"The City of Brotherly Love" and "The Cradle of the Nation"

Predict!

Discuss the following questions with your classmates.

1. The city of Philadelphia is also referred to as "the city of brotherly love." What might this nickname tell you about the people who named this city?
2. The other nickname for Philadelphia is "the cradle of the nation." A cradle is literally a type of bed in which a baby sleeps. Why might this expression be used in reference to Philadelphia?

Vocabulary Preview

From the choices that follow each pair of sentences, choose the meaning for each of the underlined expressions. You will hear the first sentence in each pair again when you listen to the recording about Philadelphia. The second sentence in each pair uses the same vocabulary in another context.

___ 1a. The area that is today Philadelphia was first settled by the Swedes in the 1630s, who <u>dubbed</u> it New Sweden.

1b. Because of her bright red hair, the neighborhood kids <u>dubbed</u> Melissa carrot-top.
    a. played
    b. blamed
    c. named

____ 2a. Following this inspiration, Pennsylvania soon became a haven for people of all religions—Jews, Roman Catholics, and others who wanted to escape the religious <u>persecution</u> in Europe.

2b. Racial <u>persecution</u> has been a serious problem throughout the history of the United States, but many Americans strive to create and live in a country equal and open to people of all colors and religious backgrounds.
    a. a situation of suffering against a specific group of people
    b. conviction in a court of law
    c. murder

____ 3a. Following the laying out of the city in 1682, Philadelphia quickly became a city of <u>commerce</u>, exporting many agricultural products to England and the West Indies.

3b. Many students come to the United States to study international <u>commerce</u>. Later, many return to their countries to run their own companies.
    a. architecture
    b. business
    c. politics

____ 4a. The shipyards were building ships of <u>exceptional</u> quality, which made it easier for traders from the city to begin exploring the riches of Europe and China.

4b. Colleen is an <u>exceptional</u> student, receiving perfect scores on all her exams.
    a. extraordinary
    b. terrible, bad
    c. curious

____ 5a. Even from colonial times there was a large population of free African Americans in Philadelphia. This allowed the city to develop into a natural center for the anti-slavery <u>movement</u> during the nineteenth century.

5b. There has been a successful <u>movement</u> in the United States to save many endangered species from extinction. Animals such as the bald eagle now have a brighter future ahead of them.
    a. going from one place to another
    b. a group involved in achieving a specific goal
    c. downfall

____ 6a. By the 1830s, Philadelphia had lost its <u>prominence</u> as a center of politics, culture, commerce, and finance. Traders preferred the large, growing port of New York.

6b. The instant <u>prominence</u> received by the sales of her new novel stunned Diana so that she had to always prepare herself mentally each time she made a public appearance to promote her book.
    a. punishment
    b. wealthy and famous
    c. being well-known and considered important

___ 7a. It's on a <u>peninsula</u> surrounded by the Delaware River to the east and south and the Schuylkill River to the west.

7b. Italy is often referred to as a boot because of its uniquely shaped <u>peninsula</u>.
  a. coastline
  b. island
  c. piece of land surrounded by water on three sides

___ 8a. "The Cradle of the Nation" has become a popular tourist attraction due to the <u>restoration</u> of historic buildings in the downtown area following the country's bicentennial celebration in 1976.

8b. Due to pollution and other damage over the years, Michelangelo's masterpiece in the Sistine Chapel has had to undergo a major <u>restoration</u>. Today, it is once again full of vivid color and detail.
  a. change
  b. causing harm to an old structure or piece of art
  c. bringing something back to its original condition

What Do You Already Know?
With a partner list three things you know about Philadelphia today.

_____

_____

_____

Notetaking Strategy 3: Anticipate.
Think of the type of lecture you will hear. Then predict the kind of information that will be given by the lecturer. For example, in a history lecture you may hear a lot of dates and names, and in a chemistry lecture you may hear a lot of formulas. If you can brainstorm about what you might hear in general about a topic before listening to a lecture on it, you can focus on the details of the lecture much more easily.

Notetaking Exercise 1
Next to each of the following topics, work with a partner to write down some examples of information you may hear in a lecture about the topic.

1. depression _____

2. English grammar _____

3. the Internet _____

4. history of Europe _____

5. impressionist painters _____

Notetaking Exercise 2

Now, write down the type of information you anticipate hearing in the following lecture on Philadelphia, Pennsylvania.

_____

_____

_____

The Main Points: First Listening

Listen to the recording once to understand only the main points.

What's the Point?

Using Notetaking Strategies 1, 2, and 3, fill in the correct answers for the following sentences. These sentences reflect some of the main points about Philadelphia.

1. Philadelphia was settled by people who ....

   ....

2. Before 1830, Philadelphia was a center of

   ....

   ....

   ....

3. Philadelphia has been a city full of people

   who ....

   ....

   ....

What Do You Remember?

Using Notetaking Strategies 1, 2, and 3, compose written answers to the following questions. Were these the types of questions you thought you would be able to answer before you heard the lecture?

1. Describe the original settlers of Philadelphia.

2. What happened in Philadelphia during the Revolutionary War?

Statue of George Washington in front of Independence Hall

Photo by Mike Bell

3. Describe the industries that thrived in Philadelphia during the eighteenth and early nineteenth centuries.

Details, Details: Second Listening

Listen again to comprehend some of the details about Philadelphia, Pennsylvania.

What Was That Again?
A. Fill in the notetaking guide that follows. Some key information has been given to you but not all of it. Fill in all the important information and details.

17th century:
    William Penn

18th century:
    Commercial trade

    American Revolution

19th century:
    Anti-slavery

    Immigration

20th century:
  Tourism

B. Now, based on your notes, answer the following questions to help you better understand
the details of the lecture.

1. The city of Philadelphia was first
    settled by _____ .
    a. Swedes and Finns
    b. people from the Quaker religion
    c. King Charles II of Great Britain
2. The residents of Philadelphia exported
    _____ .
    a. sugar to the West Indies
    b. agricultural products to Great Britain
    c. rum to Boston
3. Benjamin Franklin was a leader in
    _____ .
    a. the leather industry
    b. scientific affairs
    c. the American Revolution
4. _____ was the main commer-
    cial trading port after 1830.
    a. New York
    b. Philadelphia
    c. Pittsburgh

The Liberty Bell

Photo by Mike Bell

5. In the 1980s, Philadelphia's African American population made up _____ of
    the city's population.
    a. 14%
    b. 40%
    c. 44%

Post-listening Activities

After listening twice, you're ready to examine information included in the lecture more closely.

Discuss the Details

With a partner, discuss the answers to the following comprehension questions. Write notes from your conversation and be prepared to explain your answers to the class.

1. Discuss how industry has changed over time in the city of Philadelphia.
2. How did the railroad change Philadelphia's economy?
3. Discuss what a visitor to Philadelphia might see in the downtown area of the city. What significance do these attractions have in the history of Philadelphia?

What Really Happened?

Some of the following statements are true and some are false. Mark each either T for true or F for false. If a statement is false, correct it.

____ 1. King Charles II gave Pennsylvania to William Penn.
____ 2. Philadelphia means brotherly love.
____ 3. Benjamin Franklin was a leading shipbuilder in Philadelphia.
____ 4. The national capital was permanently established in Philadelphia following the American Revolution.
____ 5. Many anti-slavery activists met in Philadelphia.
____ 6. Philadelphia was no longer a popular port for commerce by the 1830s.
____ 7. The railroad came to Philadelphia in 1864.
____ 8. Many white residents of Philadelphia moved to the suburbs in the twentieth century.
____ 9. Philadelphia is surrounded by water on three sides.
___ 10. You can see the Freedom Bell in Philadelphia today.

Vocabulary Blitz

Word Forms

Try to figure out the correct form for each vocabulary word in the chart that follows. (Some words don't have different forms. Those are marked with Xs.)

Noun	Verb	Adjective	Adverb
XXXXXXXXXXX	dub	XXXXXXXXXXX	XXXXXXXXXXX
persecution			XXXXXXXXXXX
commerce	XXXXXXXXXXX		
XXXXXXXXXXX	XXXXXXXXXXX	exceptional	
movement	XXXXXXXXXXX	XXXXXXXXXXX	XXXXXXXXXXX
prominence	XXXXXXXXXXX		
peninsula	XXXXXXXXXXX		XXXXXXXXXXX
restoration			XXXXXXXXXXX

Now, choose the correct form for each of the following sentences.

1. The _____ people of Africa have been moving from country to country trying to find a safe place to live.
   a. persecution
   b. persecute
   c. persecuted

2. Many American airlines fly both private and _____ flights.
   a. commerce
   b. commercially
   c. commercial

3. You are an _____ healthy person!
   a. exceptional
   b. exceptionally

4. The president holds a position of _____ in the company.
   a. prominence
   b. prominent
   c. prominently

5. Florida lies on a _____ piece of land.
   a. peninsula
   b. peninsular

6. My dream house is a large _____ Victorian.
   a. restored
   b. restoration
   c. restore

Vocabulary in Context

Check your definitions from the Vocabulary Preview. Fill in each blank with the appropriate word from the following list. Remember to change the form of the word when needed.

persecution	commerce	exceptional	movement
dub	prominence	peninsula	restoration

1. Tourism and _____ are two very important industries in the United States.

2. The _____ of the old house made it look like new.

3. The _____ ability of some students to succeed remains a mystery. It is quite amazing how they can study so hard, participate in many activities, and do so well at everything!

4. In the past year, there has been a _____ to allow more immigrants into the country, although there are still some people who are against it.

5. The _____ of the enormous and elegant Statue of Liberty in the middle of New York Harbor reminds many Americans of their democratic heritage.

6. Florida is a _____, bordered by the Atlantic Ocean on the east, the Gulf of Mexico on the west, and the states of Georgia and Alabama to the north.

7. The _____ of people of the Jewish faith during World War II caused many to die from starvation. There was really no sane reason for their suffering.

8. Philadelphia has been _____ the cradle of the nation because many of the early ideals of the country were discussed there.

Writing about What You've Learned

Could your hometown be considered a "city of brotherly love"? If yes, why? If not, what nickname would you give your hometown and why? Try to use at least four of the vocabulary words learned in this chapter in your writing.

Read More about It

Read the following news article, then do the exercises that follow it.

A Mural Program to Turn Graffiti Offenders Around

Smithsonian Magazine, July, 1993, by Steven Barboza

A few hundred yards from the lazy Schuylkill River in downtown Philadelphia, three would-be Henri Rousseaus, paint in hand, climb off an embankment and set up shop in their workaday world: a **scaffold** along Route 76. In what is virtually a high-wire act above a highway, they block out expressway noise to paint a 150-by-40-foot cement wall, bringing to life a steamy jungle scene fit for the zoo a few blocks away.

scaffold
temporary platform to do work on

"It's kind of fun!" shouts Dietrich Adonis, standing 15 feet above eastbound traffic, clutching a beam with one hand and, with the other, dabbing yellow paint onto the neck of a giraffe. It joins zebras, a panda, a lion.

"Sometimes I'll take a break and watch the guys rowing in the river, watch the cars go by, and a school of ducks. It can put you in a meditative mood!" He smiles. Trucks roar by. The scaffold vibrates as if there's an earthquake.

Meanwhile, perched even higher over traffic, Jane Golden, in trademark bandanna and paint-splotched jeans, stops outlining a gracefully curving leaf to give former graffiti artist Alfredo Ramos a few pointers on creating the jungle floor.

"Right here!" she shouts, pointing to an area of dense deep green. "Just do cross-hatching—a little this way and that way." As a fuel hauler rolls by, followed by a flatbed truck, Golden demonstrates with her brush. Ramos nods. Then both fall silent, lost in their work.

The daredevil artists' so-called "Zoo" mural, visible from cars, boats, planes and trains, is one of more than 1,200 inspired by the city's collective wish to blot out graffiti. Taken together, the murals are transforming Philadelphia from a spray-painter's paradise into a respectable outdoor art gallery.

For years, graffiti writers had free rein, and the city felt powerless to overcome their scourge. In the daily press, Philadelphians were obliged to follow the legendary exploits of scrawlers, including one bold enough to write his name on an elephant in the zoo.

But today, Philadelphia has scrawl at least somewhat under control. Buildings stay cleaner, thanks to an agency the city wields as its eraser: the Philadelphia Anti-Graffiti Network. Part government agency, part social service organization, part art workshop, it not only repaints the town in richer hues, but it cleans walls, fences-off vacant lots, mobilizes neighborhood volunteers and guides youths to better futures, including art school.

In 1984, at the start of his first term, Mayor W. Wilson Goode founded the Network as an **amnesty** program for wall writers. Graffiti-fighting ranked among his top priorities, and soon after taking office he pledged to win the war of the walls. As reporters watched, he pitched in, wearing overalls as he helped to paint over a recreation center buried in scrawl.

amnesty
acting as receiving a pardon

Goode's grass-roots appeal worked. More than 130 youngsters surrendered within a year, pledging to abandon their scribbling. Through the '80s, well over 70,000 volunteers and former wall writers joined them—or were caught and stopped. Officials claim that the Network has cut back graffiti by 50 percent. Each year the organization cleans about 4,000 properties, using 5,000 gallons of city-bought paint. The cost was some $39,000 last year, compared with $150,000 a year for paint in the year when the war was at its height. Today, the Network has three basic programs: graffiti removal, mural art and art education, and youth employment. Young people get involved as volunteers, paid employees, or offenders caught wall writing and sentenced to community service by the courts.

The Network, particularly its mural division, has transformed sections of Philadelphia, lending a bit of charm to staid middle-class neighborhoods, veneering eyesores in poorer areas, and bringing new life to sites where senseless shootings had taken place. In a section of the city called "the Ozone," a mural with mournful faces serves as an epitaph for slain youngsters, their names listed in columns beneath the blood-red words "STOP THE VIOLENCE." A similar mural at Seventh Street and Susquehanna Avenue in the East of Broad area contains the names of 35 youths, most of them shot dead in the past three years. Facing this mural is another, "Peace and Unity," with a Puerto Rican flag and a Bible, driving home a plea for peaceful coexistence on the city's mean streets.

The man who leads the program is 35-year-old Tim Spencer. Hired by Mayor Goode in 1984, he had never lost touch with the Philadelphia streets of his childhood, and so was well suited to the task of putting together the Network's programs. He grew up amid gangs, watching them do battle, hearing about acquaintances killed for stupid reasons.

"I call this hell," says Spencer, driving his city-owned sedan past the East of Broad mural, then by garbage strewn lots and abandoned buildings. "We've worked extra hard over here in hell country because there's a lot of social problems and drugs—and not much hope."

Neighborhood residents appreciate the murals, some of which depict the faraway places people may wonder about but cannot afford to visit. Like giant postcards, they are windows on far prettier sights. A tropical garden sprouts from a cement wall; Mount Kilimanjaro towers majestically over rubble; scenes warm the heart on frigid days.

Working on as many as 12 projects each summer day, maybe half that in chillier weather, muralists shuttle paints and supplies and talent across the city; as the murals go up, the neighbors come out to watch art materializing on the dilapidated buildings next door. It's up to Jane Golden to find the walls and turn them into something wonderful to look at. It's also her job to get permission from owners and neighbors to paint.

"I'm a wall hunter," she laughs, jockeying her car through a city neighborhood, her beeper sounding from time to time. As she talks, she keeps her eyes peeled for potential sites. "We used to joke we were the art police—that's a good wall!" She's spotted a graffiti-scrawled building beside a vacant lot.

Today, Golden is seeking a site for a mural to be commissioned by a Philadelphia record producer who, like most businessmen, will pay for paint and materials. This 70-foot-wide wall is the side of an abandoned building; the adjacent lot is overrun by weeds. Canvassing from house to house, she rings doorbells and gets neighbors' permission, then asks three people near the street corner. All three like the idea. "I think it's a great thing," says Johnny Scott, 69, who offers to store Network paint in his cellar. Mary Watson, 83, who has lived on the street for more than 30 years, says she wouldn't mind "something decent to look at." And, in perhaps the strongest vote of confidence, Patricia Jackson, who lives down the street, tries steering Golden her way: "The 1900 block needs something done, too."

It's evident that Philadelphians like their 1,200-plus Network murals, many of which rank as unofficial landmarks; the waiting list has swelled to more than 1,500 buildings. The mural that city dwellers associate most closely with the Network is nicknamed the "Colossus of Ridge Avenue." Rising 40 feet on the side of a three-story house and overlooking a fenced-off lot stands basketball legend Julius (Dr. J) Erving. Looking sharp in a double-breasted suit, he contributes to traffic jams.

Unlike most of the murals, which are painted on-site, "Colossus" is actually a gigantic paint-by-numbers work. Young artists created it in a hotel room, dabbing millions of dots onto two-foot-square cutouts of parachute cloth that had been mapped out by California muralist Kent Twitchell. When they fastened the squares onto the wall with acrylic gel, pointillism took over, integrating the dots seamlessly. Only then did the mural make perfect sense to its painters. Some people complained that Spencer shouldn't have put the mural near "one of the worst drug corners in the city." He answered by saying, "That's where you're supposed to put it." According to neighborhood residents, the lot in front of "Colossus," once strewn with debris, stays clean and has less drug traffic.

Another mural has brought attention to a corner lot that is as big as a football field—a place where many strata of Philadelphians meet. Nicknamed "Boy," the giant work on the side of Desmond Fladger's home at North 40th Street and Powelton Avenue has been called a "Third World Statue of Liberty." "I think it's an asset to the neighborhood," says Fladger. "It has a message there—that for young black males and females alike, we all have a chance." The 72-foot-wide mural is a reproduction of Boy, with Raised Arm, an original painting by Sidney Goodman in the Franklin Mint collection. Goodman, who had conducted art workshops for the Network, offered to help with the mural of his painting.

"I was a little nervous having a fine artist like Goodman supervise my work," says Golden, who usually heads production herself and works with the community to create designs. Otherwise, the making of "Boy" was fairly typical. First, the design was divided into one-inch squares that were transformed into one-foot squares on the wall by using chalk lines. Then an overall sketch of "Boy" was drawn while Goodman supervised from the ground. The artist painted the face himself; the rest was done mainly by Network staff and crew, with neighborhood youngsters pitching in on the bottom sections.

"Boy" stands watch over the House of Clowns Car Wash, an outdoor soup kitchen, a vegetable patch and a flower garden—all on the site of a former gas station. The place is a refuge. Homeless people get free meals, and alcoholics and drug addicts earn money washing cars while they stay out of trouble, says car wash proprietor James (Mr. June) Liles. "We try to keep the ground just as beautiful as the picture," adds Liles. "And that picture has brought so much peace and harmony. I have heard church people say here it seems like you're on holy ground."

Perhaps more accurately, the mural, like others in Philadelphia, is a kind of demilitarized zone—a no-man's-land between muralists and graffitists. For the most part, scrawlers leave murals alone. But they also leave clear messages that they haven't given up the fight for control of the city's walls. "Kids write around murals—to let us know they could deface them but won't," says one former Network starlet. "It's a power struggle. We do a mural, then all of a sudden we get new graffiti—to let us know they are shadowboxing with us."

And graffiti still abounds. With ladders chained to their bikes or jutting out of car trunks, hit-and-run wall writers hunt for bare spots on which to empty several hundred cans of spray paint each month—on schools, stores, warehouses, underpasses, houses, churches, landmarks. Writers make inane proclamations on City Hall, declarations on Independence Hall. Their work even overlooks the grave of Ben Franklin.

Although there are some interesting graffiti compositions in vibrant neon colors, the great majority of graffiti are eyesores—paint sprayed onto walls in thick overlays of random scrawls. And artful or not, the owner of the wall has no say in the matter. Businesses are prime targets. The recent experience of a Philadelphia kitchen-equipment firm is typical: hit over a period of several nights, its walls and front gate were turned into a comic book. When he finished swearing, the exasperated manager got in touch with the Network, which has put his building on its mural waiting list.

Graffiti writers, who generally come out late at night, are mostly young males, although their ranks include older males and females as well. One female graffitist has made a name for herself by writing in only one color and in hazardous locations. Her style is recognizable and she signs her work; Network field representative Jonathan Heard has been trying to track her down.

A Mural of "Boy" by the Philadelphia Anti-Graffiti Network

Heard's sleuthing is often successful because he knows the world of the graffitists from the inside—in the early '70s he was among the better-known practitioners. Even after joining the Army he kept writing, scrawling graffiti on barracks walls. A lot of the writers admired him, he says, but as he grew older and became a father, he began to see himself in a new light.

After hearing of the Network's pledge of amnesty, Heard quit writing, and the local graffiti underworld lost a hero. "For the first two years I got a lot of negativity from them," he says. "It bothered me that when I was doing bad things they treated me like some kind of god, but when I started doing something good they hated me, calling me '**snitch**' and 'turncoat.' Eventually people began to see that if I could turn my life around, so could they." Now, as a field rep, he is uniquely equipped to search out writers.

snitch
someone who reports that another person is doing something wrong

Heard has his work cut out for him. Young people still seek to build "rep"—their reputations—by performing daredevil acts with cans of paint: scaling tall buildings to "tag" them with their nicknames, venturing down subway tunnels or simply being brash—like the writer who reportedly scrawled "Brisk, Catch Me" across a police van.

In Philadelphia, a dozen or so writers reign among their peers as "kings" and "queens," graffiti's royalty, who have "accumulated many properties." Graffiti writers publish their own underground magazine, *Nastie English*. A bimonthly, it contains four-color photographs of pieces on city walls, along with essays and reviews of hip-hop records. The graffiti-writing clubs meet regularly in subway stations. "We would call the pay phones to find out who was there," says Fred Scott Jr., 25, a Network volunteer who abandoned graffiti and became a computer service engineer. Writers show up at meetings clutching sketchbooks that bulge with drafts of detailed plans of attack for a night's work. The writers talk shop, laugh over "war" stories, plan "bombing" raids, then disperse in squadrons across the city, leaving their tags around town: Knife. ERX. Slice. Joker.

"We wanted to be seen," says Scott of his street days, "so somebody came up with the great idea that if we walked the same route that the buses do, the kids in the morning would see our tags. We each went different routes, probably like 12 o'clock in the morning till 3, then went home, got up at 8 so we could be to school at 9. My mother never knew I was going out in the middle of the night."

Heard and the other field reps comb the streets for local talent, even as the Network murals are being done to cover up the talents' work. The reps examine walls, trying to unmask the identities behind the mysterious tags. They visit suspected writers at home to try to persuade them to volunteer for Network duty before the police wise up to them. Often, field reps glean information from suspects by winning their confidence. They unmasked one notorious writer by first unmasking a friend of his and convincing him it was in his best interest to fink.

Field reps give their leads to a special police unit in the Juvenile Aid Division, established in 1985 to track down hard-core writers, those who had done $10,000 to $20,000 in damage. The police unit arrests 40 to 50 wall writers each year. If a Family Court judge sentences the writer to "scrub time," the writer can end up under the supervision of a Network field rep. Scrub time varies from 50 to 100 hours, depending on how much damage the writer has done.

Working alongside people sentenced to scrub time are volunteers who have been befriended in the neighborhood by reps or recruited where they live. On a typical home visit, Jonathan Heard drops in on the McCandlesses on North Third Street. As the family gathers at the kitchen table, he tries to persuade Damon and Nick, 15 and 13, to volunteer. Heard talks of the brutal life on the streets: "How would you like your mother to get a phone call saying your son's down here in the morgue with a bullet in the head? 'Cause there's people out there carrying guns. The crime rate and the death rate are people your age; they ain't just blacks dying and they ain't just Hispanics—everybody's dying."

Pouting and holding an unsigned Network form—a pledge not to write on walls—Damon fidgets, while Nick bites his fingernails. "Right now it's volunteer work, but it could lead to employment," Heard goes on. Damon asks how much time he'll have to commit. "No set time," says Heard. "I could use you one week and use your brother the next week. Take your time, read it over. Call me when you finish. I'll take you to lunch. I'll treat you. I hope you eat only hot dogs. And make sure you brush your teeth 'cause I hate bad breath." Damon breaks his cool and cracks a smile; his family laughs. "And make sure you wash your feet 'cause I hate stinky feet," Heard adds. Nick points to his younger sister, Monica: "How did you know?" Heard leaves without signing the youngsters, but he says the bullet hole part of his **spiel** will make them seriously consider joining the Network. Besides, they might have fun.

spiel
dramatized story

Most of the youngsters start out on scrubbing crews, but there are plenty of activities to move on to. The Network enrolls them in teen clubs, arranges for them to visit museums with professional artists like Sidney Goodman and signs them up for the mural program. The Network also runs a weekly art workshop, bringing an artist to Hancock Manor, a housing complex in northwest Philadelphia, for classes. Lined up at rows of easels, youngsters painstakingly paint cartoon characters, cats and other favorite subjects, transforming the lobby of the 46-unit building into a studio. The Network also sponsors the annual Clean Sweep Games, in which several hundred urban youths—teams from around the country—run races with brooms and barrels and trash bags as they polish their cleaning skills.

In the mural program, Jane Golden tries to instill a love of art but is not searching for a Michelangelo. "Let art schools do that," she says. "This is about reality, about having kids learn about discipline, responsibility in the world, and coming out of this program with some sense of their own identity, values and self-esteem, so they can go and live a normal life and not end up dead or in jail like a lot of people that they know."

The Network apparently succeeds at helping many young people find their niche. "Out of the 10,000 former wall writers who have taken the pledge not to wall write anymore, I would say that 85 percent of them are turned around—they're either holding down full-time jobs or attending art school or college, or they're in the Armed Forces," says Tim Spencer.

Some Network youngsters have honed their art skills enough to make a little money. At last count, 28 of them had sold 37 works of art for a total of $3,910. Among them was "Zoo" muralist Alfredo Ramos, who earned $90 codesigning the cover of a D.J. Jazzy Jeff and the Fresh Prince recording. And the Network spurred Fred Scott Jr. to get a college education and start a computer maintenance company. "I had a lot of energy, but I pointed it in a negative direction," he says. "The Network helped me point that energy in a positive direction." Program veteran Nelson Wynder opened a store with a partner, where he sells T-shirts he's created; another ex-writer has opened his own barber shop. At least two dozen former graffitists have gone on to art school.

The young people in the program move on, but the murals remain, treasured assets in their neighborhoods. When a site for a mural has been agreed upon, the local residents are asked for ideas. Sometimes one of them produces a photograph, which may then serve as a model. Because of this process, many of the murals reflect the values of the neighborhoods they're in. The themes sometimes include black and Latino heritage, family values, America-the-melting-pot and we-are-the-world brotherliness. Sports figures are also popular; a recently completed mural depicts the late Hank Gathers, who was a basketball star from Philadelphia.

After the choice of a theme come the hours of effort required to make the mural a reality, which can be broken down roughly into nine steps: putting up the scaffolding, scraping, whitewashing, gridding, sketching, coloring, perfecting the painting, applying adhesive and removing the scaffolding. The more talented youths, such as former graffiti writers Haisonn Shadding and Maurice Carter, work as lead artists on the crews (Carter's crew did the mural of Hank Gathers).

It's a lot of work, but gradually the young people get into it. "They'll start to paint a little and then they're hooked," says Jane Golden, "because they're out there working, and people are coming up and saying it looks great and thank you.

"And then, maybe the press comes by and does an interview, and suddenly they're heroes, sort of—only now, they're on the right side of the law."

What More Did You Learn?

Discuss the following questions, based on the previous article, with a partner. Be prepared to explain your answers to the class.

1. How does Dietrich Adonis sometimes feel while painting?
2. What is the purpose of the Philadelphia Anti-Graffiti Network?
3. Why was Tim Spencer so well suited to run the Network's programs?
4. How do the murals benefit the neighborhoods in Philadelphia?
5. What is Jane Golden's job?
6. How was "Colossus" made?
7. What message does "Boy" send?
8. What has happened to the graffiti writers in Philadelphia?
9. What is Jonathan Heard's job?
10. How do some graffiti writers earn a "rep"?
11. How does the Network find new artists?
12. If graffiti writers don't agree to join the Network, what could happen to them?
13. Once a young person joins the Network, what might he or she be doing?
14. What other activities might he or she be able to join in on?
15. What has happened to some of the former wall writers turned Network volunteers?

Analyze It

How might this type of solution to a problem work in your city? With a partner, discuss a problem common with teenagers and other young people around the world. How would recruiting teenagers to combat the problem work in your country? What might be another way to solve some of these problems?

Tell Us More about It

Prepare an oral or a written report on one of the following topics. Use the outline that follows to organize your presentation and take notes while researching.

William Penn

Quakers

King Charles II of Great Britain

shipbuilding in Philadelphia

First Continental Congress

American Revolution

Benjamin Franklin

Pennsylvania Railroad

Liberty Bell

immigration to Philadelphia

Topic:

Major points to discuss about this topic:

1.

2.

3.

4.

Details to discuss about each major point:

Major Point 1

Major Point 2

Major Point 3

Major Point 4

4 | *Honolulu, Hawaii*
"The Crossroads of the Pacific"

Predict!
Examine the pictures throughout the chapter. With a classmate, think of three reasons why people might visit Honolulu. Discuss these reasons with the class.

Vocabulary Preview
Choose the best definition for the underlined expression in each sentence. You will hear these phrases again when you listen to the recording about Honolulu.

___ 1. Honolulu is a <u>destination</u> for tourists from all over the world who want to enjoy the warmth of the tropical sun.
  a. place someone is going
  b. vacation
  c. home away from home

___ 2. Honolulu was first settled by Polynesians centuries ago, when it was given its present name, which means <u>sheltered</u> bay.
  a. circular
  b. heated
  c. protected

____ 3. In the 1820s, Protestant <u>missionaries</u> from New England arrived in Honolulu with the purpose of converting the Hawaiian people to Christianity.
a. people who teach and spread a religion
b. people who want to learn religion
c. people who settle in a new place

____ 4. Many Americans of Asian <u>descent</u> became strong leaders of Honolulu's politics and businesses.
a. origin
b. children
c. family

____ 5. Many high-rise apartment buildings and luxury hotels were built along the ocean side to <u>accommodate</u> tourists.
a. house
b. show
c. eliminate

____ 6. U.S. military <u>personnel</u> and their families make up about fifteen percent of Honolulu's population.
a. commanders
b. visitors
c. employees

____ 7. Diamond Head, an <u>extinct</u> volcano, is at the eastern end of the city, making a serene backdrop for the Honolulu skyline.
a. large
b. no longer existing
c. active

____ 8. Most tourists stay in the Waikiki Beach area of the city, but <u>developers</u> are now building resorts in other parts of the city to lessen the overcrowding in Waikiki.
a. government
b. hotel workers
c. builders

What Do You Already Know?
With a partner list three things you know about Honolulu today.

_____

_____

_____

Notetaking Strategy 4: Abbreviate.

Abbreviate terms you use often. Some terms you may use a lot are:

and = +, &	definition = def	with = w/
for example = e.g. or ex	therefore = Δ	information = info
	one, two, three, etc. = 1, 2, 3, etc.	because = bec

Create your own system for abbreviations, but make sure that you remember the code you used in your abbreviated notes so you can understand your notes when you need to study later on.

Notetaking Exercise: What Else Can You Abbreviate?

A. Look at the following paragraph on Las Vegas, Nevada. Abbreviate as much as possible but only enough so that you can still understand the meaning of the information.

> With a population of 258,000, Las Vegas, Nevada, is a city known worldwide for its nightclub entertainment and gambling casinos. Located in southeastern Nevada, about two hundred miles east of Los Angeles, California, Las Vegas is a year-round desert resort. The city entertains millions of guests each year, is a major convention center in the United States, and is the center for commercial and mining activity in the southwestern region of the country.

_____

_____

_____

_____

_____

_____

B. Exchange your abbreviated paragraph with a classmate. Critique each other's work. Do you understand the abbreviations your partner used? If not, explain your methods of abbreviation to each other.

The Main Points: First Listening

Listen to the recording once to understand only the main points.

What's Most Important?

A. Using Notetaking Strategies 1, 2, 3, and 4, make note of the most important information contained in the lecture on Honolulu, Hawaii, and any details supporting that information.

Important point #1:

Important point #2:

Important point #3:

Important point #4:

B. Compare your notes with a classmate's notes. Did you miss anything? Write in some of the missing information and be prepared to listen for it during the Second Listening.

What Do You Remember?

A. From your notes, create two comprehension questions based on the main ideas of the lecture on Honolulu, Hawaii.

Question 1.

Question 2.

B. Exchange questions with a classmate. Answer the questions your classmate created. Did you take enough notes to answer the questions?

Details, Details: Second Listening

A. Listen again to comprehend some of the details in the lecture about Honolulu, Hawaii. Fill in the missing information in your notetaking outline.

Waikiki Beach

B. Fill in each blank with the correct answer. Refer to your notes, if needed.

1. One nickname for Honolulu is ....

2. The Polynesian name, Honolulu, means ....

3. King Kamehameha I lived in Honolulu from .... to ....

4. By the end of the 1800s, ... became a successful crop for Hawaiian farmers.

5. People from Japan and China came to Hawaii in order to ....
....

6. Hawaii was made the .... state of the United States in ....

7. By 1992, ... tourists were visiting Hawaii each year.

8. Pearl Harbor is ....

9. The former capitol building of Hawaii is called ....

10. The average temperature in Hawaii in the month of February is ....

Post-listening Activities

After listening twice, you're ready to examine information included in the lecture more closely.

Putting the Pieces Together
Compare notes with a classmate to answer the following comprehension questions.

1. Describe the early history of Hawaii.
2. Why is Hawaii such a popular tourist destination?
3. Describe the presence of the United States Armed Services in Hawaii.

Talking about It
Eric is telling Mary about the trip he took to Honolulu last month. With a partner, fill in Eric's lines.

Mary: Hey there, Eric! I heard you traveled all the way to Honolulu last month. What was your favorite part of the trip?
Eric:

Mary: Oh, I've always wanted to see that. It sure seems beautiful in pictures. What else did you see?
Eric:

Mary: Oh, yeah. Isn't that the famous army base? My favorite would be that gorgeous beach. What is that called again?

Eric:

Mary: That's it. Sounds like you had a good time. Did you learn anything about Honolulu's history?
Eric:

Mary: What a funny name for a king! But, how did the Europeans find Hawaii?
Eric:

Mary: Wow, I've learned so much about Hawaii from you that I think I'm going to plan a trip there soon.

Vocabulary Blitz

Word Forms

Try to figure out the correct form for each vocabulary word in the chart that follows. (Some words don't have different forms. Those are marked with Xs.)

Noun	Verb	Adjective	Adverb
destination	XXXXXXXXXXX	XXXXXXXXXXX	XXXXXXXXXXX
		sheltered	XXXXXXXXXXX
missionaries/	XXXXXXXXXXX	XXXXXXXXXXX	XXXXXXXXXXX
descent/		XXXXXXXXXXX	XXXXXXXXXXX
	accommodate		
personnel	XXXXXXXXXXX		XXXXXXXXXXX
	XXXXXXXXXXX	extinct	XXXXXXXXXXX
developer/			XXXXXXXXXXX

Now, choose the correct form for each of the following sentences.

1. This umbrella will _____ you from the rain. (sheltered)

2. Where is the _____ that was just built? (missionaries)

3. Mary claims she is _____ from royalty. (descent)

4. Are these the best _____ you could find? (accommodate)

5. Where is the _____ department? (personnel)

6. Is the Tasmanian Devil _____?(extinct)

7. The Jones's are living in that new _____ . (developer)

Vocabulary in Context

Check your definitions from the Vocabulary Preview. Fill in each blank with the appropriate word from the following list. Remember to change the form of the word when needed.

destination	extinct	missionary	descent
sheltered	personnel	developer	accommodate

1. Today, there are many _____ working in various parts of the world,

   helping the people to improve their literacy and standard of living while teaching some

   new religious ways.

2. Although we spent two nights in Minneapolis, San Francisco was our final

   _____ .

3. Many different types of dinosaurs roamed the earth in prehistoric times, but they

   became _____ during the Ice Age.

4. Over the past twenty years, _____ have really built up the area around the

   East Coast town of Hyannis, Massachusetts, on Cape Cod.

5. As a little girl, Amy's parents tried to keep her from danger, but in reality, they

   _____ her from many of the positive things of childhood.

6. I hope we have good _____ on our vacation to Tahiti. I would really hate

   to get stuck in an old, noisy hotel.

7. The original settlers of the United States were mainly of British _____, but

   immigrants from other countries arrived later in our country's history.

8. The _____ of most American companies rely heavily on their employers

   for benefits, including expensive health insurance.

Writing about What You Learned

Some people consider Hawaii "paradise on Earth." What is paradise to you? Is it a person, place, thing, or feeling? Describe your idea of paradise here. Try to use at least four of the vocabulary words learned in this chapter in your writing.

Read More about It

Read the following news article, then do the exercises that follow.

Hawaii Families Resettle on Land

Associated Press, March 16, 1997, by Meki Cox

It's a simple stone house without running water or electricity on a generous slice of land that runs from the dormant volcano Haleakala to the sea on the island of Maui.

But for Donna Simpson and her 9-year-old daughter, Kawehi, this is their dream home. Here they can hunt and farm and gather just as their Hawaiian ancestors did centuries ago.

By the end of the year, 125 families will have resettled 23,000 acres of barren land known as Kahikinui, set aside by Congress in 1921 for native Hawaiians but never developed or distributed.

"My ancestors are from Kahikinui. That's why we want to go back home," said Simpson, a single parent.

The families will live primitively under the old Hawaiian-style land concept, known as ahupuaa, in which the land, which runs from the forest to the ocean, provides people with game, building materials, water and garden plots.

Kahikinui is part of 200,000 acres Congress reserved under the Hawaiian Home Lands Act. A waiting list was started with the names of all people who had at least 50 percent native Hawaiian blood. Many people died while waiting decades for the state to put in roads, running water and other improvements, as required by law. The list today has 16,000 names.

Now, for the first time, the state is letting a native Hawaiian group develop land by themselves, said Aric Arakaki of the state Department of Hawaiian Home Lands, which administers the 200,000 acres.

A chronic shortage of money has slowed state plans to develop the land, most of which is in the poorest, most remote areas where the costs of preparing land for **homesteading** is highest, Arakaki said.

But some Hawaiians say they will be satisfied with living on bare land.

"Hawaiians just want to be caretakers of the land again," said Mo Moler, spokesman for the native group Ka Ohana O Kahikinui, some 30 people who have volunteered to get the land ready. The name means "The Family of Big Tahiti." Kahikinui is thought to be the place where the original Polynesians came ashore in Hawaii.

"These people don't want to live in the city, but in the country where their ancestors used to live," he said. "This is about going back to the basics, culturally, physically and spiritually."

A year-long survey has uncovered thousands of clues that a large population of Hawaiians once lived on the area. Among items found were religious shrines, house and burial sites, fish bones and stone tools, Arakaki said.

Under the new program, the state is letting native Hawaiian families lease undeveloped areas for $1 per acre annually for 99 years.

homesteading
claiming a piece of land for one's home

Water will be collected from mountain fog in catchment systems. Energy will eventually come from solar power, Moler said. A transmitter will provide communications.

The homes will use solar heating, composting toilets, wind energy and water-saving techniques, he said.

If the program proves successful, Arakaki said, the Home Lands department will lease additional plots of undeveloped trust land to the next native Hawaiians on the waiting list.

"Old-timers now drive by and say to me how amazed they are that Kahikinui has life again," Moler said.

What More Did You Learn?

Discuss the following questions, based on the previous article, with a partner. Be prepared to explain your answers to the class.

1. Why are these families being allowed to move to Kahikinui?
2. Why is Kahikinui being developed now?
3. What is ahupuaa?
4. What is special about the site of Kahikinui in Hawaiian history?
5. How will water be provided to those living in Kahikinui?
6. If this program is successful, what does the Home Lands Department hope to do?

Analyze It

The people who move to Kahikinui are going to have a lot of hard work ahead of them. Help them out. Make a ten-year plan of all the things they'll need to do to develop their new community. Think of all the things necessary in your life, and add them to your plan.

Tell Us More about It

Prepare an oral or a written report on one of the following topics. Use the outline that follows to organize your presentation and take notes.

Polynesians	volcanoes
Captain William Brown	Pearl Harbor
King Kamehameha I	tourism in Hawaii
U.S. military in Hawaii	Waikiki Beach

Topic:

Major points to discuss about this topic:

1.

2.

3.

4.

Details to discuss about each major point:
Major Point 1

Major Point 2

Major Point 3

Major Point 4

Side Trip

Hawaii Volcanoes National Park

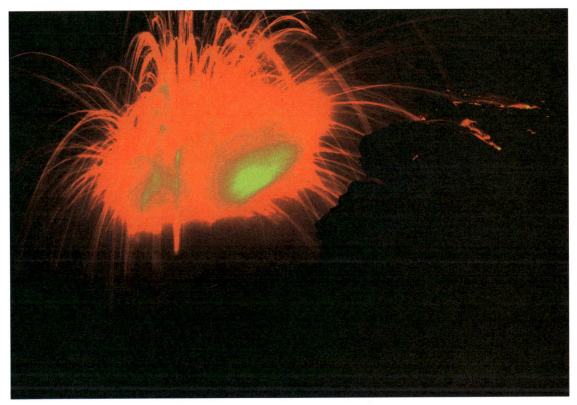

Lava exploding as it hits the ocean on the Big Island

Predict!

With a partner, make a list of everything you know about volcanoes. What kind of destruction have these mountains done around the world? Do you know what is different about the volcanoes in Hawaii?

Key Expressions

Following are some expressions and names that might help you better understand the lecture on Hawaii Volcanoes National Park.

| Aloha | Kilauea | lava | Mauna Loa |
| Madame Pele | Halemaumau | | |

Taking It All In

Listen to the mini-lecture twice. On your own piece of paper take notes of all the important information you hear. Then answer the following questions using your notes.

1. What is the nickname for the island of Hawaii?
2. How many volcanoes are on Hawaii?
3. When did the most recent eruption on Kilauea begin?
4. Why is it one of the best studied volcanoes in the world?
5. What happened in April of 1987?
6. What does the name Mauna Loa mean?
7. Why is Mauna Loa distinctive?
8. Who is Madame Pele?
9. How do the natives try to make her happy?
10. What will happen if you take a lava rock home with you?

A truck trapped in cooled lava

5 | *Los Angeles, California*

"Tinseltown"
and "The City of Angels"

Predict!

Examine the pictures throughout the chapter and use your existing knowledge of Los Angeles, California. With a classmate, think of three reasons why people might visit Los Angeles. Discuss these reasons with the class.

Vocabulary Preview

From the list that follows, choose the meaning for each of the underlined expressions. You will hear the first sentence in each pair again when you listen to the recording about Los Angeles, or L.A. as it is commonly known. The second sentence in each pair uses the same vocabulary in another context.

a. characterized by violence or physical aggression
b. popular and in style
c. rule politically
d. became strong and did very well
e. changed from one religious belief to another
f. an examination of two or more things, places, or people

____ 1a. They farmed the land and <u>prospered</u> over the next fifty years.
      1b. The family <u>prospered</u> after they won a million dollars in the lottery.
____ 2a. The Native Americans who originally populated the area of Los Angeles were <u>converted</u> by the Spaniards to Catholicism and forced to become slaves.
      2b. When he married Mary, Mark <u>converted</u> to her religious faith.
____ 3a. The city was later captured by the United States during the Mexican War in 1846. Since then, it has been <u>governed</u> by the United States, but a large number of its inhabitants are still of Mexican descent.
      3b. The president <u>governs</u> the entire country.
____ 4a. Then it was a small, <u>rough</u> cow town that averaged one murder each day.
      4b. Matt is a <u>rough</u> little boy. He gets into fights almost every day.
____ 5a. It was still a small city in <u>comparison</u> to those in northern California.
      5b. A lot of people make a <u>comparison</u> between Boston and San Francisco because both are small, charming cities.
____ 6a. Many of the most popular tourist attractions include homes of movie stars in the <u>fashionable</u> city of Beverly Hills, which borders Los Angeles, and the movie studios throughout the area.
      6b. Red is very <u>fashionable</u> this year; everyone is wearing it.

What Do You Want to Know?
Compose two questions you would like answered by the time you finish this chapter about Los Angeles, California. Present your questions to the class to see if anyone knows the answers.

Question 1.

Question 2.

Notetaking Strategy 5: Pick out details.
Pick out important details, such as dates, names of people, places, and things, definitions, and examples of general ideas. Group the corresponding information together so you know that it is related. For example:

1876 ⇨ Philly, Cent. Expo ⇨ bright spot

The Main Points: First Listening

Listen to the recording once to understand only the main points.

What's the Point?

A. Use the following lecture outline to take notes on Los Angeles, California. When you listen the first time, listen for the main ideas and as many details as you can, but don't worry too much about the details until the second listening.

Spanish arrival and original settlers

Easterners arrive

After oil discovery

Movie industry

Earthquakes

City today

B. Compare your notes with a classmate's notes. Did you miss anything?

What Do You Remember?

A. From your notes, create two comprehension questions based on the main idea of the lecture on Los Angeles, California.

Question 1.

Question 2.

B. Exchange questions with a classmate. Answer the questions your classmate created. Did you take enough notes to answer the questions?

Details, Details: Second Listening

A. Listen to the recording again for important details about Los Angeles, California. Fill in the details in your notetaking outline that you missed during the First Listening.

A scene from a television set in Los Angeles

B. Answer the following questions.

1. Why is Los Angeles known as the "City of Angels"?
2. Who were the original inhabitants of Los Angeles?
3. Who arrived there and later ruled these original inhabitants?
4. How did Los Angeles become an American city?
5. Why did many easterners go to Los Angeles?
6. Why are highways around Los Angeles always filled with traffic?
7. Why did the movie industry become established in Los Angeles?
8. Name some of the ethnic groups who live in Los Angeles.

Post-listening Activities

After listening twice, you're ready to examine information included in the lecture more closely.

What Happened When?
Put the following statements in chronological order by placing a number (1, 2, 3, etc.) next to each. Then, next to each statement, write the year in which the incident occurred.

___ The movie industry was attracted to California because of the physical characteristics of the landscape. Year_____

___ Los Angeles experienced its last large earthquake. Year_____

___ Many people traveled to California in search of gold. Year_____

___ The Native Americans who originally lived in the area were forced into slavery by the Spanish. Year_____

___ The railroad arrived in Los Angeles. Year_____

___ Los Angeles was settled by the Spanish near the Indian village of Yang-na. Year_____

___ Mexico claimed California as its own, after declaring its independence from Spain. Year_____

___ Oil was discovered in the Los Angeles area. Year_____

What Really Happened?
Pretend that you are writing home about a visit you made to Los Angeles. You only have enough paper to tell the important details of your trip. Using the lines that follow, write your letter.

Dear Mom and Dad,

_____

_____

_____

_____

_____

_____

_____

_____

_____

_____

Love,

_____

Vocabulary Blitz

Word Forms

Try to figure out the correct form for each vocabulary word in the chart that follows. (Some words don't have different forms. Those are marked with Xs.)

Noun	Verb	Adjective	Adverb
	prosper		
/	convert		XXXXXXXXXXXX
/	govern		XXXXXXXXXXXX
		rough	
comparison			
	XXXXXXXXXXXX	fashionable	

Now, choose the correct form for each of the following sentences.

1. What a _____ occasion! (prosper)

2. Mike is a _____ to Buddhism. (convert)

3. What kind of _____ exists in Thailand? (govern)

4. The little girl played _____ with her new toy. (rough)

5. Try to _____ the two dogs. (comparison)

6. We arrived at the party _____ late. (fashionable)

Vocabulary in Context

Check your definitions from the Vocabulary Preview. Fill in each blank with the appropriate word from the following list. Remember to change the form of the word when needed.

| prosper | convert | govern | rough |
| | comparison | fashionable | |

1. After all the hard work she put into her business, it began to _____ . By the end of the year, she was rich.

2. Ronald Reagan _____ the United States for eight years.

3. Life in the United States today is much better in _____ to what life was like for the early settlers of the country.

4. Life in some parts of New York City can be _____ , but some people survive the turbulence and end up doing well in life.

5. Why should I _____ to your way of thinking? Your ideas don't make any sense, but mine do.

6. Miniskirts were very _____ during the 1960s.

Writing about What You've Learned

Los Angeles, California, is known as the home of the movie industry. Describe the best American movie you have ever seen. Why do you like this movie? Give examples to support your statements. Try to use at least four of the vocabulary words learned in this chapter in your writing.

Read More about It

Read the following news article, then do the exercises that follow it.

A Rags-to-Riches Tale Right out of Hollywood; Miramax Deal Means Big Bucks for Bartender

USA Today, April 16, 1997, by Elizabeth Snead

One month you're a struggling musician, pouring beers for would-be writers and dying-to directors in a dusty saloon.

The next you sign a multimillion-dollar deal with Miramax for your first film script, *The Boondock Saints.* You will also direct, though you've never directed so much as traffic before, and pick the film's stars. And you'll do the soundtrack, featuring your fledgling band performing songs you've written.

Top talent agency William Morris signs you (and your band), and during negotiations with Miramax, Paramount Pictures hands you a two-picture writing deal for $500,000.

Sound like a dream? Meet Troy Duffy, 25, the guy this just happened to, now the most envied man in Hollywood.

And to put a nice frothy head on things? Miramax honcho Harvey Weinstein will buy J. Sloan's, where Duffy tended bar, and make Duffy co-owner.

"People ask me how I'm handling this," says the chain-smoking, tattooed Duffy, downing a noontime brew at a wooden booth in the dark Melrose Avenue saloon. "How do you handle winning the lottery?"

Miramax's press release about the March 28 deal sputters with enthusiasm. "Troy is a unique, exciting new voice in American movies. We are thrilled that he has come on board."

Duffy's deal sounded so unique that some industry insiders mistook the trade stories that ran March 31 as April Fools' pranks.

"It is unprecedented," concedes Kirk Honeycutt, who reported the story in the *Hollywood Reporter* two weeks ago. "This is one of the most unusual deals I've encountered, what they're giving away to a complete neophyte. Add the bartender bit, and it's a fabulous success story."

Duffy didn't plan on making movies; he was focused on music. He says the Saints script was a **fluke** after he'd seen "one too many bad movies."

fluke
accidental success

He asked a pal for some scripts to check the format. Then he frantically wrote *Saints,* the tale of two religious Irish brothers, Connor and Murphy McManus, who decide to rid society of evil by killing bad people.

Duffy saved up each month to rent a computer for $150 a week. After a few months, he handed the completed script to longtime **chum** Chris Brinker, formerly with New Line Cinema, who passed it to producer pals. "And the rest," intones Duffy, "is history."

chum
close friend

The Weinstein brothers, Miramax co-chairs Harvey and Bob, devoured the script during Oscar week, as their other unconventional talents Anthony Minghella (*The English Patient*) and Billy Bob Thornton (*Sling Blade*) were nabbing their first gold statues. When Harvey Weinstein met Duffy, he told his wife, "That's the future of the movie business."

Coincidentally, Duffy sports the alternative young Hollywood look: goatee, shorn head, baseball cap. "He does have that Billy Bob look," Honeycutt admits. His love life also sounds slightly Thorntonesque. His wife of three years, Lisa Marie Janis, filed for divorce a few months ago. The name of his high-school girlfriend, Kerri, is tattooed on his arm, above designs he liked from an old Led Zeppelin album cover.

While it's not the norm for a novice screenwriter to retain such control on his first project, it is becoming more common as studios **ferret out** new faces like good ol' boy Thornton and former video store clerk Quentin Tarantino, who directed and co-wrote the Oscar-winning *Pulp Fiction* (1994).

ferret out
search out and find

Harvey Weinstein revels in making Hollywood's moguls shake their well-gelled heads at his audacity. "They started shaking their heads at *sex, lies and videotape,* and they shook their heads at *Sling Blade*," Weinstein says. "That's my job, to make heads shake and make great movies."

Five producers, with credits that include *Michael*, *Dazed and Confused,* and *Blown Away*, are involved in *Saints*. All met Duffy at the bar.

Rob Fried (former CEO at Savoy Pictures, now executive producer for TriStar's *Godzilla*) isn't worried that Duffy can't cut the celluloid mustard. "He shows clarity of vision and is a good communicator of ideas with a lot of confidence," Fried says. "With the proper support team, I think he can pull it off."

That Duffy is a virgin director doesn't scare Miramax either. "We'll surround him with the best technicians, and he already has terrific producers," Weinstein says. "Besides, Troy knows the script better than anyone."

Duffy also knows the film industry, not from loitering on studio lots but from observing from behind the bar. He quickly saw that confidence is key in Hollywood's high stakes game.

"Be prepared. Know what you want. Don't be afraid to ask for it," says Duffy, who dropped out of the pre-med program at Colorado State University, then knocked around Los Angeles for three years putting together his band, The Brood, with brother Taylor, 24.

That's why when he was asked by studio representatives during negotiations what directing experience he had, he shot back, "I watch movies."

"It's funny," he recalls. "No one really questioned it. I just said, 'I want this, I want this,' and they were like, 'We finally got someone who knows what he wants.'"

Duffy learned early to fight for what he wanted. He was second oldest of five kids in a big Irish family living in Kensington, a suburb of Exeter, N.H., 45 miles north of Boston.

It was a rough childhood for a skinny kid, he says, and he suffered his share of black eyes and bloody knuckles in neighborhood fights. He recalls, "Mom left a steak in the fridge for us every day."

Brawls aside, he was an avid reader thanks to Dad, then an English teacher who made all the kids read novels and give monthly reports.

"I gave him (James Joyce's) *Portrait of the Artist as a Young Man* when he was 14 because I knew he was ready for it," says Robert Duffy, his father. "When I listened to his report, tears ran down my face because he had found the heart and soul of the book."

Just two months ago, Duffy received a care package of Structure sportswear from Dad. Now he can afford Armani. But it's doubtful he'll be hitting

Rodeo Drive's boutiques. First thing he wants is a car ("a '49 Merc") so he won't have to keep hitching rides with pals and taking the bus to his studio meetings.

Saints, with a reported $10 million to $15 million budget, will start filming in Boston this fall. Name actors are lining up for a look at the script.

"It's amazing. Every big agency has opened their rosters to us," says Duffy, who has had to turn down actors he admires (such as Brad Pitt) because "they aren't right for this project."

Casting, directing, doing the soundtrack; won't this be incredible pressure?

"Nah," says Duffy. "Pressure was coming here five nights a week pouring beer, hauling kegs. That's pressure. This isn't pressure; it's a dream come true."

So is becoming part owner of J. Sloan's (built in 1918 and looks it), which with Weinstein's purchase is sure to become a new Hollywood hangout. The Weinstein brothers are partners with Robert De Niro in five restaurants such as Manhattan's Nobu and the Tribeca Bar and Grill.

Duffy recalls the night Harvey Weinstein first walked in. "He sits down and he's not in Industryland anymore. My friends treat him like a regular guy, not a god. So he says, 'I love this place. How much is it?'"

"I haven't had beer by the pitcher in 15 years," Weinstein recalls. "It was incredible."

Duffy says with a smile, "Harvey had been hanging out at too many face bars," referring to L.A.'s array of pretty-people places.

The courtyard at the J. Paul Getty Museum in Malibu, California

What More Did You Learn?

Discuss the following questions, based on the previous article, with a partner. Be prepared to explain your answers to the class.

1. What was Troy Duffy doing for a living before his big break in Hollywood?
2. What is *The Boondock Saints* about?
3. What's so unusual about Duffy's deal with Miramax?
4. Who is Duffy similar to among novice screenwriters?
5. Why is Rob Fried so impressed with Duffy?
6. How did Duffy learn about the film industry?
7. What did he learn about it?
8. What was Duffy's childhood like?
9. How did Duffy come to appreciate good writing?
10. Why did Harvey Weinstein like J. Sloan's so much?

Analyze It

Instant success and overnight fame are very difficult changes to get accustomed to. In Hollywood, it can be even more difficult. Troy Duffy is relatively young and has had a whole new world dropped at his doorstep. With a partner, make a list of advice for Troy so that fame and success don't go to his head. What dangers will he need to avoid? How can he best take advantage of his success?

Tell Us More about It

Prepare an oral or a written report on one of the following topics. Use the outline that follows to organize your presentation and take notes while researching.

Yang-na tribe of Native Americans
Felipe de Neva
Spanish presence in California
California gold rush
earthquakes

Latin influence in California
smog
the movie industry
Hollywood
Beverly Hills

Topic:

Major points to discuss about this topic:

1.

2.

3.

4.

Details to discuss about each major point:

Major Point 1

Major Point 2

Major Point 3

Major Point 4

6 | *Miami, Florida*
"The Magic City"

Predict!

Look at the pictures throughout the chapter and consider your own knowledge of Miami, Florida. What kind of place do you think Miami is to visit? How does it appear different to some of the places you've learned about so far? How does it appear similar?

Vocabulary Preview

From the list that follows, choose the meaning for each of the underlined expressions. You will hear these phrases again when you listen to the recording about Miami.

a. lengthened
b. a large number coming into a particular place quickly
c. arrived in
d. houses
e. different

f. produce
g. area of a major city and its surrounding suburbs
h. people whose wealth is more than a million dollars

____ 1. While the city itself has a population of only 370,000 people, the <u>metropolitan</u> area of Miami has a population of almost two million.

____ 2. The Spanish explorer Ponce de Leon first <u>set foot in</u> Miami in 1513.

____ 3. The East Coast Railroad was <u>extended</u> to Miami as a result of urging by the pioneer settlers in the region.

____ 4. At that time, there were not many more than a few <u>dwellings</u> near the abandoned Fort Dallas, but soon the new railroad encouraged progress in the area, attracting curious people from the northern United States.

____ 5. Men called "Binder Boys" stood on the street corners selling inexpensive real estate. Thousands of people turned into <u>millionaires</u> overnight from real estate purchases.

____ 6. The <u>diverse</u> groups that reside in Miami, including white Americans, Caribbean islanders, and Latin Americans, were attracted there for various reasons.

____ 7. This group has grown from an <u>influx</u> of 300,000 refugees who arrived in the area shortly after Fidel Castro took power in Cuba in 1959.

____ 8. More than ten million tourists visit the Miami area each year. They <u>generate</u> over sixty percent of Miami's economic activity.

What Do You Want to Know?

Compose two questions you would like answered by the time you finish this chapter about Miami, Florida. Present your questions to the class to see if anyone knows the answers.

Question 1.

Question 2.

Notetaking Strategy 6: Note what is emphasized.

Write down whatever the speaker emphasizes. Listen for key words and phrases that indicate emphasis. Some of those words may be:

actually, moreover, finally, however, primarily, in fact, such as,
the most important, the basic idea, the chief cause, or any superlative.

Notetaking Exercise

A. Underline words and phrases that indicate emphasis in the following paragraph.

> By the 1830s, Philadelphia had lost its prominence as a center of politics, culture, commerce, and finance. Traders preferred the large, growing port of New York. Still, Philadelphia's economic activity was boosted once again when the Pennsylvania Railroad completed a line to Pittsburgh, Pennsylvania, from Philadelphia in 1854, allowing for increased regional trade. After the American Civil War, a war between the North and the South, Philadelphians and other Americans were drawn to the excitement of the Centennial Exposition in 1876, one of the first great world's fairs, whose main focus was the display of U.S. technological advances.

B. Now, compare your work with a classmate's work. Did you underline the same words and phrases?

The Main Points: First Listening

Listen to the recording once to understand only the main points.

What's the Point?

A. Use the notetaking outline that follows and listen for the main ideas of the lecture on Miami.

Location and climate

Early history

19th century

20th century

1930s and 1940s

1960+

Tourist attractions

What Do You Remember?

A. From your notes, create two comprehension questions based on the main idea of the lecture on Miami, Florida.

Question 1.

Question 2.

B. Exchange questions with a classmate. Answer the questions your classmate created. Did you take enough notes to answer the questions?

Details, Details: Second Listening

A. Listen again for the important details of the lecture about Miami, Florida.

B. Mark the following statements T for true or F for false. Be prepared to correct the false statements.

____ 1. The metropolitan area of Miami has a population of 370,000 people.
____ 2. Lake Okeechobee is northeast of Miami.
____ 3. Henry Flagler owned a hotel in Miami.
____ 4. A real estate "boom" occurred in the 1930s.
____ 5. A hurricane hit Miami in 1926.
____ 6. Beginning in the 1940s, Miami attracted many older settlers from the western United States.

___ 7. Approximately 300,000 Cuban immigrants arrived in the Miami area in 1959.

___ 8. The Dade County Art Museum is in the Everglades National Park.

___ 9. Miami Beach lies just to the east of the city of Miami.

___10. Two percent of Miami's permanent residents are involved in the hotel and restaurant business.

Post-listening Activities

After listening twice, you're ready to examine information included in the lecture more closely.

What Really Happened?
You are spending the week in Miami. Write a brief journal entry describing your first day there.

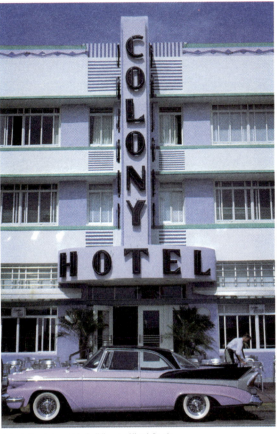
A typical art deco style building on Miami Beach

Dear Diary,

_____

_____

_____

_____

_____

_____

_____

_____

_____

_____

_____

_____

_____

_____

Vocabulary Blitz

Word Forms

Try to figure out the correct form for each vocabulary word in the chart that follows. (Some words don't have different forms. Those are marked with Xs.)

Noun	Verb	Adjective	Adverb
	XXXXXXXXXXX	metropolitan	XXXXXXXXXXX
XXXXXXXXXXX	set foot in	XXXXXXXXXXX	XXXXXXXXXXX
	extend		XXXXXXXXXXX
dwelling/		XXXXXXXXXXX	XXXXXXXXXXX
millionaire/	XXXXXXXXXXX		XXXXXXXXXXX
		diverse	
influx	XXXXXXXXXXX	XXXXXXXXXXX	XXXXXXXXXXX
	generate	XXXXXXXXXXX	XXXXXXXXXXX

Now, fill in the correct form of the word or expression in parentheses in the following sentences.

1. Miami is a beautiful _____ . (metropolitan)

2. I will give you an _____ on your final paper if you promise to do a good job on it. (extend)

3. Are these well-constructed _____ .(dwelling)

4. This is a _____ dollar deal we are working on. (millionaire)

5. Having _____ in your areas of interest is important to becoming a well-rounded individual. (diverse)

6. This factory can _____ two hundred cars a day. (generate)

Vocabulary in Context

Check your definitions from the Vocabulary Preview. Fill in each blank with the appropriate word from the following list. Remember to change the form of the word when needed.

metropolitan	set foot in	extend	diverse
influx	millionaire	dwelling	generate

1. The _____ of the nineteenth century had a certain charm that builders are unable to capture today, especially the ornate decoration of the Victorian-style buildings.

2. The population of the United States includes people from _____ backgrounds and cultures.

3. The lotteries held in many states can turn middle class people into _____ overnight.

4. Christopher Columbus first _____ the New World in 1492.

5. An _____ of immigrants from all around the world made the United States a melting pot of culture.

6. A lot of controversy was _____ over the issues in the last presidential campaign.

7. The Los Angeles _____ area includes many of the suburbs, including Burbank and Pasadena.

8. The government has decided to create an _____ of the main highway so that it reaches more people.

Writing about What You Learned

Miami was first explored by the Spanish. Who were the early settlers of your home city? Briefly describe the early history of your city. Try to use at least four of the vocabulary words learned in this chapter in your writing. (You may need to go to the library to research this question.)

Read More about It

Read the following news article, then do the exercises that follow it.

Miami's Language Gap Widens: City's Rich in Culture, but Divided

USA Today, April 3, 1992, by Deborah Sharp

Few things better capture Miami's ethnic divisions than this city's long-simmering fight over language: English vs. Spanish.

In the years since Castro seized Cuba, Miami has transformed from a quiet Southern burg to Latin American mecca. Language and cultural divisions have grown with the city.

But the 1990 Census marked a turning point. It found that fully half of the city's 358,548 residents say they have trouble speaking English—possibly the highest proportion in any large U.S. city.

"Everyone is in their own little group: the Haitians in their group, the Spanish in theirs, the Anglos in theirs," says Sandra Laurin, 21, a Miami-Dade Community College student.

Adds classmate Nicole Allen, 20: "Language is a big barrier. It's so hard to communicate with everybody, you just don't bother."

Although the ethnic stew makes Miami one of the most culturally rich cities in the country, the language gap also widens cultural barriers, sometimes leaving behind anger and misunderstanding.

Language is a hot topic in Miami, a sure bet for radio talk show hosts looking for a flood of furious callers. Frustrated Anglos—with bumper stickers reading "Will the Last American Out Please Bring the Flag?"—have left in droves.

But Hispanics—a majority here—are equally frustrated. Many feel Anglos should be able to speak some Spanish.

Nicaraguan immigrant Pedro Falcon, 30, is learning English and wonders why more people won't try to learn his language. "Miami is the capital of Latin America," he says. "The population speaks Spanish."

What's happening in Miami, says University of Chicago sociologist Douglas Massey, is what happened in cities such as Chicago at the beginning of the century: Then, as now, the rate of immigration exceeded the speed with which new residents learned English, creating a pile-up effect in the proportion of non-English speakers. "Assimilation into English is a slow process, whereas immigration is fast," he says.

Massey expects the city's proportion of non-English speakers to rise with continuing immigration. But he says that "doesn't mean in the long run Miami's going to end up being a Spanish-speaking city." Instead, he believes bilingualism will prevail.

"If you look at the elite Cubans really running the show, they all speak English," he says. "Miami's an international city for commerce in South America, and to move in that world successfully, you need to speak English and Spanish."

The Dade County school system spends $80.9 million a year in its refugee program to educate children who cannot speak English.

But in the meantime, language and cultural flare-ups make headlines: The Hispanic community was outraged last year when an employee at the Coral Gables Board of Realtors lost her job for speaking Spanish at the office.

In 1989, protesters swarmed Publix supermarket after a cashier was fired for chatting with a friend in Spanish.

And now, a heated dispute between the Cuban community and the *Miami Herald* is visible in Spanish-language advertisements on buses that read "I don't believe the *Herald.*"

Herald Publisher David Lawrence Jr. doesn't believe language is behind the dispute, but notes the language gap is "a challenge and an opportunity. The key to making this community work, the key to making any community work, is obviously communication. While lots of people, including myself, work hard to learn Spanish, part of being successful is being able to communicate in English."

In Miami's Little Havana—where Spanish is the background chatter in store after store—Jorge Cascudo, 68, says he has never felt disadvantaged because he speaks only Spanish.

"For me, it's no problem. I would have liked to learn English, but I had no time. I was always working."

Cuban-born Maria Sierra, 34, sees language as a bridge in the community, not a barrier: "I can get along with everybody. I even speak a little Creole for the Haitian people."

What More Did You Learn?

With a partner, mark the following statements T for true or F for false, based on what you read in the article about Miami. Be prepared to correct the false statements.

___ 1. Miami is a mecca for Haitians.

___ 2. One-third of Miami's residents have trouble speaking English.

___ 3. The language barrier leads to misunderstanding between language groups.

___ 4. Some Spanish speakers think others should learn their language.

___ 5. Immigration and assimilation are both happening quickly in Miami.

___ 6. Douglas Massey thinks Miami will be a Spanish-speaking city in the future.

___ 7. Most Cuban leaders know English and Spanish.

___ 8. A lot of money is being spent to teach Miami's schoolchildren how to speak English.

___ 9. Some employers encourage Spanish at work.

___ 10. Communication will lead to understanding between the different language groups.

People enjoying Miami Beach

Analyze It

Work with a partner to answer the following questions.

1. Based on what you learned in the lecture on Miami, and what you read in the previous article, why do you think the language barrier has become such a big problem in Miami?

2. Draw up a plan to help the city of Miami solve the language barrier problem. Make a list of suggestions and be prepared to explain how each suggestion should be implemented.

Tell Us More about It

Prepare an oral or a written report on one of the following topics. Use the outline that follows to organize your presentation and take notes while researching.

Calusa tribe of Native Americans	hurricanes
Tequesta tribe of Native Americans	the Great Depression
Lake Okeechobee	art deco
Ponce de Leon	Cuban Americans
Fort Dallas	Everglades National Park

Topic:

Major points to discuss about this topic:

1.

2.

3.

4.

Details to discuss about each major point:
Major Point 1

Major Point 2

Major Point 3

Major Point 4

7 | *Las Vegas, Nevada*
"The Gambling Capital of the World"

Predict!
Discuss the following questions with your classmates.

1. Examine the pictures in the chapter. Does Las Vegas look like a fun city to visit? Why or why not?
2. What type of things would you do if you visited Las Vegas?

Vocabulary Preview
From the list that follows, choose the meaning for each of the underlined expressions. You will hear the first sentences in each pair again when you listen to the recording about Las Vegas. The second sentence or set of sentences uses the same vocabulary in another context.

a. referring to something that is possible in the future but doesn't exist now
b. controlling influence
c. member of a group of organized criminals
d. risking money or other things on playing games
e. a place in the desert where there are trees, grass, and water
f. made to seem less important or smaller in size
g. something passed on or left behind by someone after he or she dies
h. a source of great wealth
i. exactly and conveniently

     1a. Because of the <u>dominance</u> of the <u>gambling</u> industry in Las Vegas, it is hard to believe there is much history associated with it.

____ 1b. A <u>gambling</u> addiction is difficult to overcome because it most likely involves the loss of a lot of money.

____ 1c. The New York Yankees' <u>dominance</u> in baseball this year is not surprising, but it was expected that the Chicago Cubs would do well, too.

____ 2a. But they almost ran out of water, so Armijo sent a young Mexican scout named Raphael Rivera to search for an <u>oasis</u>.

2b. Walking through the desert, the travelers spotted a beautiful <u>oasis</u> where they filled up on their supply of water.

___ 3a. The group thought Las Vegas was a good place to stop on their way from Salt Lake City, Utah, to San Bernardino, California, because it was located <u>perfectly</u> between the two cities.

3b. Claudia is <u>perfectly</u> suited for the part of Juliet; she is the right age and a wonderful actress as well.

___ 4a. Still standing in that area today is the Victory Hotel, built in 1910, <u>overshadowed</u> by the modern Golden Nugget Hotel and Casino on North Main Street.

4b. The Empire State Building <u>overshadows</u> most other buildings in New York, with the exception of the World Trade Center, New York's tallest building.

___ 5a. Benjamin Siegel, the <u>gangster</u> and casino owner, is the one who is most associated with the history of Las Vegas and the gambling industry.

5b. Once a <u>gangster</u>, Peter had decided he wanted to lead a lawful life, so he got a good job at a bank.

6a. He saw the city as a <u>potential</u> <u>gold mine</u> for gambling.

___ 6b. As a <u>potential</u> candidate for the office of president of the United States, she was devastated to discover that she didn't have enough money for a campaign.

___ 6c. Acting can be a <u>gold mine</u> for only a few people; most would-be actors will never make enough money to live comfortably.

___ 7a. Although Siegel was shot in his Beverly Hills, California, home in 1947, his <u>legacy</u> lives on in fancy casinos like Caesars Palace and the Sands.

7b. Martin Luther King, Jr., left a <u>legacy</u> in the field of civil rights for African Americans.

What Do You Want to Know?

Compose two questions you would like answered by the time you finish this chapter about Las Vegas, Nevada. Present your questions to the class to see if anyone knows the answers.

Question 1.

Question 2.

Notetaking Strategy 7: Paraphrase.

Paraphrase the details of a lecture. Do not write down what the speaker says word for word. Find another way of expressing the same information given in the lecture, but keep the same meaning. Sometimes what you paraphrase may be shorter than the original information, and sometimes it will be of equal length. If examples are given, you should write them down exactly as you hear them, so there is no misunderstanding when you review your notes later.

Notetaking Exercise

Look at how the example paragraph is paraphrased. Then, read through paragraph B and paraphrase it in a similar way.

A. Example

By the 1830s, Philadelphia had lost its prominence as a center of politics, culture, commerce, and finance. Traders preferred the large, growing port of New York. Still, Philadelphia's economic activity was boosted once again when the Pennsylvania Railroad completed a line to Pittsburgh, Pennsylvania, from Philadelphia in 1854, allowing for increased regional trade. After the American Civil War, a war between the North and the South, Philadelphians and other Americans were drawn to the excitement of the Centennial Exposition in 1876, one of the first great world's fairs, whose main focus was the display of U.S. technological advances.

1830s ⇨ Philly no longer center of politics, business, finance ⇨ these moved to NY
But ⇨ 1854 Penn. RR came from Pittsburgh to help economy
1825+ ⇨ Philly industries incl. ⇨ coal, textiles, iron, steel, shipbuilding, shoes
1876 ⇨ world's fair came to city, displayed advances in U.S. technology

B. At the time of its founding, Los Angeles was only a small settlement of forty-four people, but it grew under Mexican rule as the temporary capital of California. Named El Pueblo de la Reina de Los Angeles (the Town of the Queen of the Angels) by the Spanish governor of California, Felipe de Neva, it was later shortened by the inhabitants to simply Los Angeles, meaning "the angels." The first settlers were a mixture of Spaniards, Native Americans, people of mixed blood, and African Americans, many of whom were women and children. They farmed the land and prospered over the next fifty years.

The Indians who originally populated the area of Los Angeles were converted by the Spaniards to Catholicism and forced to become slaves. They helped the Spaniards build religious missions along the coast of California. With the Native American slaves dying in large numbers and the Spanish government involved in too many other overseas projects, Mexico declared its independence from Spain in 1821 and claimed California as its own. The city, however, was later captured by the United States during the Mexican War in 1846. Since then it has been governed by the United States, but a large number of its inhabitants are still of Mexican descent.

_____

_____

_____

_____

_____

_____

_____

_____

The Main Points: First Listening

Listen to the recording once to understand only the main points.

What's Most Important?
A. List the most important information contained in the lecture on Las Vegas, Nevada.

B. Compare your notes with a classmate's notes. Did you miss anything?

What Do You Remember?
A. From your notes, create two comprehension questions based on the main idea of the lecture on Las Vegas, Nevada.

Question 1.

Question 2.

B. Exchange questions with a classmate. Answer the questions your classmate created. Did you take enough notes to answer the questions?

Details, Details: Second Listening

Listen again to comprehend some of the details about Las Vegas, Nevada.

What Was That Again?
A. As you listen, fill in the following notetaking guide:

A. Las Vegas today:

B. History

Indians

Antonio Armijo

Mormons

Farming

Railroad

Gambling

Hoover Dam

Benjamin Siegel

B. Now, using your complete notes, answer the following questions to help you better understand the details of the lecture.

1. Las Vegas is located in _____ Nevada.
   a. northwestern
   b. southwestern
   c. southeastern
2. The Pueblo tribe of Native Americans visited the area of what is today Las Vegas in about _____.
   a. 30 B.C.
   b. 300 B.C.
   c. 3 B.C.

3. The first expedition of white men to enter the Las Vegas area was led by
   _____ .
   a. Antonio Armijo
   b. Brigham Young
   c. Raphael Rivera
4. What happened in 1855? _____
   a. A group of traders from New Mexico wandered through the area of Las Vegas.
   b. Benjamin Siegel opened his first hotel in Las Vegas.
   c. A group of Mormon missionaries came to the area of Las Vegas.
5. The Mormons eventually moved to _____ .
   a. Los Angeles
   b. Utah
   c. Santa Fe
6. After the railroad was built through Las Vegas, settlers arrived hoping to get rich from
   _____ .
   a. gambling
   b. water production
   c. mining
7. Gambling was made legal again in 1931 because _____ .
   a. there was a decline in the success of mining
   b. to bring more tourists to the area
   c. to help pay for easy divorces
8. Benjamin Siegel built the first luxury hotel in Las Vegas, the _____ .
   a. Sands
   b. Victory Hotel
   c. Flamingo Hotel

Post-listening Activities

After listening twice, you're ready to examine information included in the lecture more closely.

Putting the Pieces Together
Form four groups. Each group should only answer one of the following comprehension questions based on the lecture about Las Vegas. When your group has completely answered the question, one person from each of the four groups should join a different group. Present your answer to your new group. Be prepared to answer any possible questions.

Group 1
Describe the expedition made by Antonio Armijo.
Notes:

Group 2
Who were the Mormons and what did they do in the Las Vegas region?
Notes:

Group 3
Describe the history of gambling in Las Vegas.
Notes:

Group 4
Who was Benjamin Siegel? Why was he famous?
Notes:

What Really Happened?
Tony is confused about his visit to Las Vegas. He is getting all the facts wrong when he tells his friend William about the trip. Correct his errors.

Hey, William, did you know that I just got back from Las Vegas, Nebraska? It's a great place for gambling, but the casinos are located a little bit outside of downtown. Can you believe I even got the chance to visit the first major casino ever built? It is called the Golden Nugget Hotel and Casino and is located on the Las Vegas Highway. I was so excited about this early piece of Americana that I found out more about Las Vegas's history. Did you know it was founded in 1729 by Native American men from Mexico? It was named Las Vegas because of the dry vegetation that was found there. People came from all around the United States after 1921 when laws against gambling and raising quick horses were repealed. I really liked Las Vegas, especially the stories about Boy Seabird, the first prominent casino owner, who killed himself in his Bedford, California, home.

Vocabulary Blitz

Word Forms

Try to figure out the correct form for each vocabulary word in the chart that follows. (Some words don't have different forms. Those are marked with Xs.)

Noun	Verb	Adjective	Adverb
dominance			
		gambling	XXXXXXXXXXX
oasis	XXXXXXXXXXX	XXXXXXXXXXX	XXXXXXXXXXX
			perfectly
XXXXXXXXXXX	overshadow	XXXXXXXXXXX	XXXXXXXXXXX
gangster	XXXXXXXXXXX		XXXXXXXXXXX
	XXXXXXXXXXX	potential	
gold mine	XXXXXXXXXXX	XXXXXXXXXXX	XXXXXXXXXXX
legacy	XXXXXXXXXXX	XXXXXXXXXXX	XXXXXXXXXXX

Practice with Word Forms

Now, choose the best word form for each of the following sentences.

1. The Greeks _____ ancient culture for hundreds of years.
   a. dominance
   b. dominated
   c. dominant
2. He thought he could _____ the money and win; he never thought he'd lose though.
   a. gambling
   b. gambled
   c. gamble
3. She is the _____ person to teach that class!
   a. perfection
   b. perfect
   c. perfectly
4. She has the _____ to be a great actress.
   a. potential
   b. potentially
   c. potentiality

Vocabulary in Context

Check your definitions from the Vocabulary Preview. Fill in each blank with the appropriate word from the following list. Remember to change the form of the word when needed.

dominance	gambling	oasis	perfectly	overshadow
gangster	potential	gold mine	legacy	

1. Tina fit in _____ with Mike's friends. Everyone loved her.

2. Many people become addicted to _____. As a result, they may lose all of their money.

3. The World Trade Center _____ the rest of the buildings in the city. This is because it is the tallest building in New York.

4. *The Godfather* was a movie about a family of _____ involved in organized crime.

5. The founding fathers of the United States of America left a _____ of freedom and liberty for Americans of future generations.

6. The New York Yankees baseball team maintained its _____ within the league. For the second straight year the team won the World Series.

7. The discovery of oil in Texas led some people to believe there was a _____ there.

8. The men were lost in the desert, walking for miles in search of water. Finally they came upon an _____ .

9. Even at the age of four, Mozart showed great _____ in making music.

The Las Vegas Strip lighting up the desert sky

Writing about What You've Learned

Many people who go to Las Vegas are addicted gamblers. Other addictions people might have are to cigarettes, alcohol, chocolate, and even shopping. What is the worst addiction a person could have and why? Try to use at least four of the vocabulary words learned in this chapter in your writing.

Read More about It

Read the following news article, then do the exercises that follow it.

The Rise and Fall of "Shoeless Joe" in Las Vegas

International Herald Tribune, April 19,1995, by Dave Gardetta

If the following story of the rise and fall of a gambler reads like a movie script, it may be because its setting is Las Vegas, a town that recently began taking its cues from Hollywood instead of its own sleazy past. It also may have something to do with its protagonist's striking resemblance to **Popeye**, or simply the fact that the movie and video rights are already owned by Steve Wynn, CEO of Mirage Resorts Inc. and the best-known Maryland parlor operator turned millionaire casino owner on the Vegas strip.

Popeye
popular cartoon character

The outline, as related in hushed whispers and boisterous bar conversation by dealers and waitresses and fellow players, goes like this:

On Sunday, April 2, a barefoot man who looked to be in his 80s entered the Treasure Island hotel and casino. He cashed his $400 Social Security check at the house bank and walked with the aid of a metal cane to a blackjack table.

At Treasure Island, bets at the blackjack tables start at $5 and go as high as $10,000, and it was quite possible that the old man, who fellow gamblers assumed was homeless because of his appearance, could have lost his entire monthly pension on one hand. That didn't happen. He started playing 21 and winning. And winning and winning.

Drinks are free at the 21 tables, and the man started off ordering a Jack Daniel's and Coke plus four Macanudo cigars. Such an order is called "Bubba-style" in Las Vegas, a phrase that might also describe the man, who identified himself simply as "Joe." At the table, he was grouchy and, when he was losing, emitted a steady stream of profanities in the direction of the dealer.

Joe made a memorable sight, with his small head, pink and hairless, his pinpoint lizard eyes, his thin, wide mouth showing teeth that looked like twin rows of cigarette butts—white and yellow and brown-tipped.

In the beginning, Joe took breaks between hands, walking frequently to the rest room, causing hotel guests to stare. He brought in a takeout dinner of pork chops and threw the bones on the carpet. One player from Vernon, New York, who sat next to Joe while he was betting $5,000 a hand, said he was later astonished to see Joe standing at a urinal in his bare feet.

That was before Joe started winning big, before his government check had turned into $900,000 in chips by Thursday, April 7, and then passed the million dollar mark. It was before the casino supplied him with a complimentary room, clothes, security guards and a limousine, and before casino owner Wynn bought the rights to his story for $10,000. Wynn's pal, Kevin Costner, was said to be present at the signing, and Costner's production company confirmed he was at Treasure Island at that time.

Then, as luck tends to do at the gaming table, Joe's changed. He started losing. Betting as furiously as ever, he is now said to be down to around $60,000 (as of Saturday, he was still playing).

These details, most of which are unverifiable since neither Joe nor the casino will speak to the press, have proved remarkably accurate to the extent they could be checked.

Fact: Last week, Joe was betting several $5,000 hands at a time.

Fact: He was accompanied at all times by several plainclothes security guards supplied by the hotel.

Fact: He had a suite to which he retired between gambling bouts, and a limousine, which he took out on jaunts.

Fact: He had in his pocket a contract for the film and video rights to his story.

Fact: He was still swearing.

Even if the staff of Treasure Island were talking to the press about Shoeless Joe—which they are adamantly not doing—it would be difficult to discern just who is the man currently enjoying perhaps the most incredible streak of luck in Las Vegas history. Many locals say he's homeless, but others claim he is just an old man who lives month to month on government assistance.

A dealer at the Golden Nugget remembers seeing Joe being removed from that casino for his profanity at the table a few weeks ago, but that seems to be as far back as the man's known history stretches.

Everyone in Treasure Island seems to know about Joe. The elderly women with processed hair playing Volcano and Haywire and Quartermania have heard of his luck. The slot cowboys playing Jackpot Jungle and 4th of July tell the story of Joe instructing his limo driver to take him to a local park one evening, where he spent the night sleeping on a bench.

The waitresses wearing pink and purple and yellow at the Battle Bar and the bartenders in black at the Gold Bar can discuss in detail his gambling skills. They say he is a fairly good player, although he is known to **veer** wildly from accepted strategy: When dealt two 10s, Joe will invariably split them instead of resting on 20.

veer
turn

It is said that his winnings went as high as $1.3 million before he started losing. He is said to have bought two $50,000 certificates of deposit at a nearby bank, then cashed them two days later at a substantial penalty.

When Shoeless Joe plays at the top of his form, he is known to play several $5,000 hands at a time. He never tips dealers. When another player suggested he leave a tip after a big win, he replied, "When I lost $100,000, the dealer didn't tip me."

There are not many tales like Joe's in Vegas—stories of big wins built on such a small investment. Locals remember the gentleman who walked into a casino with $25,000 in a suitcase, put it all on red at a roulette table and a while later walked out with $250,000. They speak of a pit boss from the Golden Nugget who strolled over to the Mint casino one night with $200 and built it up to $78,000 before losing the money, his job, his car and his fiancee.

The most frequent theme in conversations about Joe is his recklessness, which made him a big winner and now threatens to make him a big loser. Most gamblers assert that, in Joe's place, they'd have stashed away a million and quit when they lost the rest. It is this belief that keeps Las Vegas thriving. Joe's story provides hope for the dreamers at the tables, who in his place would have known better.

After spending days attempting to uncover Shoeless Joe's "system," casino security finally gave up and started comping him. Casinos do this for big winners in the hope of keeping them playing until the casino gets its money back.

Treasure Island typifies the new Las Vegas. Thirty stories high, it opens like a pink conch shell onto the Strip. The hotel's entrance is an imitation 17th-century sea village named Buccaneer Bay, complete with **faux wisteria**, a lagoon, a pirate ship and British Man of War stocked with young actors in beards and long tresses. A wooden boardwalk leads out to the sidewalk, which is also made of wood.

faux wisteria
fake type of plant

Treasure Island is the kinder, gentler appearance of Las Vegas that Steve Wynn is credited for creating. It has more to do with Mickey Mouse than the Rat Pack and Bugsy Siegel, and it's one of many new hotels that cater to families with wholesome shops, restaurants and shows. A homeless man with a filthy mouth doesn't fit into this town's new script, and perhaps this is part of the reason Treasure Island is so close mouthed about its big winner.

"I bet I know what you're calling about: the homeless man," cried a woman who answered the phone before passing a reporter on to the public relations department, which was more reticent. "No one from the hotel will have a comment on this," read Wynn's eventual statement to the *Washington Post*. "It is improper for us to talk about our customers."

Shoeless Joe represents an outlaw image the city is trying to shake, the guy who gets one shot at the end of his life and then blows it. His story is more film noir than family values, and it likely will come to a close on what Hollywood calls a "downbeat" ending.

Joe's story may turn out to be interesting not because of the money involved, but because it reveals Las Vegas stripped of its pirate shows and its new roller coasters and volcanoes that erupt every 15 minutes along the Strip. Despite all the accolades this town has received for its new family style, it is still a city built on losers.

"I've got to go to the bank," Joe told his guard Thursday, and the little gnome with the cigar walked out of the casino while his guard called for the limo. Approached by a reporter, Joe announced gruffly that he couldn't talk to us about his life or his luck at the casino because Steve Wynn had already bought the rights.

"Here, you want to see it?" Joe asked, pulling a printed contract out of his pants pocket. "They gave me $10,000. I can't talk to you. Where'd you say you're from?"

"The *Washington Post*."

"Can't talk to you. What do you want to give me, money?"

"No, only fame."

"There's only fame in it?"

"That's right."

"Naw, don't want to talk to you."

And retrieving his contract before the name on it could be discerned, Las Vegas's newest legend waved his cigar, withdrew into his stretch limo and disappeared into the blinding desert sun.

What More Did You Learn?
Discuss the following questions, based on the previous article, with a partner. Be prepared to explain your answers to the class.

1. What does the article tell you about Joe's past?
2. Describe Joe physically.
3. After Joe started winning big, what happened to him?
4. Describe some of Joe's erratic behavior.
5. What is "the new Las Vegas"?
6. Why does Joe have an outlaw image in Las Vegas?
7. Why wouldn't Joe talk to the reporter from the *Washington Post*?

Analyze It
In groups of three or four, analyze Joe. Give him a background. Where did he come from? What happened in his life to bring him to Las Vegas? Take notes when talking with your group and be prepared to explain your analysis to the class.

Looking down on the Hoover Dam

Tell Us More about It

Prepare an oral or a written report on one of the following topics. Use the outline that follows to organize your presentation and take notes.

Pueblo tribe of Native Americans
Old Santa Fe Trail
Colorado River
Mormons
Prohibition
Benjamin Siegel
Hoover Dam
mining in the Nevada

Topic:

Major points to discuss about this topic:

1.

2.

3.

4.

Details to discuss about each major point:
Major Point 1

Major Point 2

Major Point 3

Major Point 4

Side Trip

The Grand Canyon

View of the Grand Canyon

Predict!

How much do you know about the Grand Canyon? With a partner make a list. Listen for items on your list during the lecture.

Key Expressions

Following are some expressions and names that might help you better understand the lecture on the Grand Canyon:

Colorado River	Garcia Lopez de Cardenas	John Wesley Powell	rim

Taking It All In

Listen to the mini-lecture twice. On your own piece of paper take notes of all the important information you hear. Fill in the missing information in each statement.

1. The Grand Canyon is located in the state of ....

2. It is famous for its ...., ...
   .... and ....

3. Garcia Lopez de Cardenas was the first .... to view the canyon in
   ....

4. In 1919, the Grand Canyon became .... so it
   could ...., ...
   .... and ....

5. The oldest rocks in the canyon are ....

6. One way of seeing the canyon from below is by ....
   ....

7. The view from the rim has gotten more spectacular due to ....
   ....

8. ....
   prove prehistoric occupation by Native
   American tribes.

9. It is important to bring plenty of
   .... and ....
   if you plan to hike down one of the
   many canyon trails.

View of the Grand Canyon

Photo by Mike Bell

8 | *Montréal, Québec*
"The City of One Hundred Belfries"

Predict!
Discuss the following question with your classmates.

Look at the pictures throughout this chapter. How do you think Montréal is different from other cities in North America?

Vocabulary Preview
Choose the best meaning for each of the underlined expressions. You will hear these phrases again when you listen to the recording about Montréal.

_____ 1. Maisonneuve and his group called their village Ville-Marie and built a <u>sturdy</u> fortress of logs, and later stone, to protect themselves from the frequent attacks by the native peoples of the area.
   a. strong
   b. weak
   c. paper

___ 2. The leaders wanted the city to grow so much that they actually fined bachelors who did not take a wife within two hours after the women <u>disembarked from</u> their ships.
   a. got off
   b. got on
   c. sailed away

___ 3. A man's fur trading license could have been taken away if he didn't choose a bride, leading to a lack of <u>livelihood</u>!
   a. death
   b. income
   c. life

___ 4. Montréal was taken over by the British in 1760 after the French and Indian War, which <u>pitted</u> the French, and the natives who fought with them, <u>against</u> the American colonists and the British.
   <u>pit against</u> means:
   a. be in opposition against
   b. make a hole in
   c. win against

___ 5. Montréal continued to grow and safely <u>guarded</u> its original French heritage.
   a. eliminated
   b. saved
   c. killed

___ 6. Ice hockey is <u>second nature</u> to most young Quebecers, along with rich food, to help get them through the <u>bone-chilling</u> winters.
   <u>second nature</u> means:
   a. outdoors
   b. easily learned
   c. involving trees
   <u>bone-chilling</u> means:
   a. very, very cold
   b. not so cold
   c. almost warm

What Do You Want to Know?
Compose two questions you would like answered by the time you finish this chapter about Montréal, Québec. Present your questions to the class to see if anyone knows the answers.

Question 1.

Question 2.

Notetaking Strategy 8: Use a system of organization.
It is common to write down notes in random order during a lecture and, then, after the lecture, to forget how these random words and phrases relate to each other. One way to make sure you'll understand the relationship of the information is to draw lines or arrows to connect the related ideas.

For example:

Vancouver—Natives ⇨ arrive@500B.C.
⇧——fished, hunted, gathered
fur traders—arrived 1820s ⇨ ended native lifestyle

Notetaking Exercise

Using all of the notetaking skills you have learned so far, and incorporating Notetaking Strategy 8, organize the following portion of the lecture on Vancouver.

With the discovery of gold in the 1850s, the native people were almost permanently dislodged. While not all of the new European settlers found riches in Vancouver, many did remain to cash in on the abundant salmon in the area waters. Known as the settlement of Granville, the area boasted many great natural resources, but the terrain was so rugged that it did not attract a great number of additional settlers over the following twenty years. But by 1886, there were twenty-five hundred settlers, with half as many natives, and three hundred wooden houses. On April 6 of that same year, Granville was incorporated as a city and had its name changed to honor Captain Vancouver, the man who first charted the area. However, with ample kindling in its structures, the new city was ripe for the fire that consumed it in twenty minutes on June 13. But the spirit of the new Vancouverites overcame this tragedy and the city began to rebuild within days of the fire. It was also the year that welcomed the arrival of the Canadian Pacific Railroad and led to the city's growth by leaps and bounds; just twenty-five years later, the number of people who resided in the Vancouver metropolitan area had risen to over one hundred thousand.

The Main Points: First Listening

Listen to the recording once to understand only the main points.

What's the Point?
Write down the main ideas next to the dates given. Listen only for the most important information during the first listening, but write down as many significant details as you can.

I. 1535

II. 70+

III. 1642

      Daughters of the king

IV. 1760

      a. 1774

V. 1809

      1830s–40s

      1892

VI. 1967

      1976

VII.

      Parti Quebecois

      Culture/climate

What Do You Remember?

A. From your notes, create two comprehension questions based on the main idea of the lecture on Montréal, Québec.

Question 1.

Question 2.

B. Exchange questions with a classmate. Answer the questions your classmate created. Did you take enough notes to answer the questions?

Details, Details: Second Listening

Listen again to comprehend some of the details about the lecture on Montréal, Québec.

A. Listen again to the lecture on Montréal, Québec. This time listen especially for the details that you were not able to write down the first time you listened and for those details that are not directly associated with the dates given in your outline.

B. Mark the following statements T for true or F for false, based on what you heard in the lecture on Montréal. Correct any statements that are false.

____ 1. Montréal was founded by the British.

____ 2. The first permanent settlers called the island Mont Réal.

____ 3. The "daughters of the king" were brought over to Montréal to marry the eligible single men of the city.

____ 4. The railroad started bringing people to Montréal during the 1630s.

____ 5. Many Montréalers speak three languages.

Political graffiti in Montréal

____ 6. Expo '67 celebrated the new technology of Canada.

____ 7. French Quebecers have tried three times to create an independent Québec nation.

____ 8. Young Montréalers generally learn to play ice hockey.

Post-listening Activities

After listening twice, you're ready to examine information included in the lecture more closely.

Putting the Pieces Together
Form four groups. Each group should only answer one of the following comprehension questions based on the lecture about Montréal. When your group has completely answered the question, one person from each of the four groups should join a different group. Present your answer to your new group. Be prepared to answer any possible questions.

Group 1
Describe the early settlers of Montréal.
Notes:

Group 2
What happened in eighteenth-century Montréal?
Notes:

Group 3
Describe Montréal today.
Notes:

Group 4
What is the Parti Quebecois and what have they been doing in the Province of Québec?
Notes:

Talking about It

Charlie went to Montréal and is telling his friend Ben about his trip. He has left out some of the details. Fill in what Charlie has forgotten.

Hey Ben! I just got back from Montréal the other day. What a great town that is! It is filled with history everywhere. Did you know that it was one of the earliest explored areas in North America? A guy named _____ first explored it in 1535 and then this other guy named Samuel de Champlain spent time there in _____ . But the first time people decided to settle there permanently was in _____ when a group of _____ came over from France. The leaders of the town even brought over _____ from France for the men to _____ . Then, in 1760, the _____ took over the city, and it's been run by them ever since. Over the last twenty years, the French population of the city has tried a couple of times to secede from Canada because they've felt like they've been losing their _____ .They haven't been successful, but the votes have been very close. It must be really neat to live in a place like Québec. Maybe you could come with me next time, Ben.

Vocabulary Blitz

Word Forms

Try to figure out the correct form for each vocabulary word in the chart that follows. (Some words don't have different forms. Those are marked with Xs.)

Noun	Verb	Adjective	Adverb
	XXXXXXXXXXX	sturdy	
	disembark from		XXXXXXXXXXX
livelihood	XXXXXXXXXXX	XXXXXXXXXXX	XXXXXXXXXXX
XXXXXXXXXXX	pit against	XXXXXXXXXXX	XXXXXXXXXXX
	guard		XXXXXXXXXXX
second nature	XXXXXXXXXXX	XXXXXXXXXXX	XXXXXXXXXXX
XXXXXXXXXXX	XXXXXXXXXXX	bone chilling	XXXXXXXXXXX

Now, choose the correct form for each word in parentheses in the following sentences.

1. His _____ came in handy when we had to move the heavy box. (sturdy)

2. The point of _____ is Los Angeles. (disembark)

3. The heavily _____ bank had been the target for a bank robber the previous

   day. (guard)

Vocabulary in Context
Check your definitions from the Vocabulary Preview. Fill in each blank with the appropriate
word from the following list. Remember to change the form of the word when needed.

sturdy	disembark from	livelihood	pit
guard	second nature	bone chilling	

1. He earned his _____ in sales; although he didn't make much money at it,

   he was very happy.

2. Playing the flute was _____ to Anna. She seemed as if she were born to

   play music.

3. That is a _____ table. It is holding 500 pounds of stuff, and it doesn't even

   appear to be weakening.

4. This weather is so _____ that I think we need to kindle a fire.

5. Cats like to _____ their food so no one else can get at it.

6. The football game next Saturday _____ New York against Detroit.

7. I hate _____ an airplane because you have to wait such a long time while

   the people in front of you gather their belongings together.

Writing about What You've Learned

Montréal is closely associated with its French culture, snow, and ice hockey. What is your city well known for? Write a short composition describing this. Try to use at least four of the vocabulary words learned in this chapter in your writing.

A typical Montréal street

Read More about It

Read the following news article, then do the exercises that follow it.

Hints of Warmth; Social Aspects in a 1950s Montréal Neighborhood

Canadian Geographic, July 1996, by Rosa Harris-Adler

There is a moment, every spring throughout Canada, when decay and rebirth **duke it out**—and rebirth wins. Along Outremont Avenue, in the heart of the quiet middle-class Montréal **neighbourhood** for which the street is named, the ripening buds on the centenarian maples, anxious to grab that moment, explode in unison as soon as there's a hint of sustained warmth. Then the trees relax for the summer, forming a shady, shuddering arch over the road. That's when the seasoned folk, who live in the turn-of-the-century, red brick duplexes and the **verandahed**, single-family brownstones, finally pull out the wicker porch furniture and settle into it when the sun sets. They sit out front. The street is stately, but the backyards are pebbly, muddy. Little can be coerced to grow beneath the gnarly old chestnuts and lilacs that, with their girth and their cheap perfume, dominate like fearsome old aunts.

It is just such a late-spring evening, circa 1958. Carole Paradis, a bored, lanky, nine-year-old redhead, is sitting on her back stairs overlooking her barren backyard patch. She can hear a steady clink-clink from around the corner as the on-duty firemen play horseshoes in an empty grass lot opposite their station on Saint-Just Avenue. Around another corner, kids on Laviolette Avenue are batting **birdies** into the trees with badminton racquets. A father whistles, a signal that it's time for his young daughter to come home for supper.

It's turning sultry with the dusk: if the local kids can finagle a dime out of their parents, soon they'll be making their way down Outremont to Bernard Avenue. They might stop to browse at the corner store to see if the latest adventures of Superman have arrived. Portly Louie, the owner, tolerates the kids because of their parents' trade, but he arches one eyebrow and plays with his mustache as they thumb his comics with sticky fingers. They leave without buying, as usual. Their real destination is Robil's, where 10 cents will get you a one-scoop, sickly-sweet ice cream cone.

Robil's consists of one high counter—you have to get up on tiptoes to give the soda jockey your money—and naugahyde-covered booths. But no one hangs out here. The store is lit up like **Alcatraz** after a prison break. Fluorescent lights glare down from the ceiling, hissing and spitting in harmony with the houseflies buzzing round them.

Sometimes kids are entrusted with ice cream orders from their parents. They walk gingerly, carrying the extra cones in egg cartons with holes punched in them.

Carole Paradis, meanwhile, is expertly putting a bolabat through its paces while a mangy black-and-white cat follows the motion with his eyes.

---

duke it out
fight to win

neighbourhood
British English spelling of neighborhood

verandahed
having a type of patio

birdies
object that is hit in the game of badminton

Alcatraz
prison on an island in San Francisco Bay

Soixante et un, soixante-deux, Carole says absently, as the little red ball attached by an elastic string returns to the balsa-wood bat with a thwak. She is pretending not to notice the giddy skip-rope chants of the young girls next door, to whom her eyes are wistfully drawn.

The girls she is watching are the younger Gledhill sisters, Ginny, 9, and Charmiane, 11. "My mother told me," the sisters recite in a monotone singsong as they jump, "if I was goody, that she would buy me a rubber dolly." They are aware of Carole's scrutiny, but they don't quite know what to do with it: there is an unspoken protocol in these parts that a Gledhill does not play with a Paradis any more than a Harris plays with a Tremblay. The English and French children, equally represented in this boomer community, find one another exotic, a curiosity. The English go to Protestant schools, the French to Catholic. Relations between them are genuinely cordial, genuinely distant. Mingling seems not to be an option. Kids will skip a house or two just to find another kid in their language group. It is just the way things were.

Outremont has aged with reasonable grace, although the grass lot where the firemen played has been paved and parking meters have been put up. Robil's has evolved into a **gelato parlour** with hanging plants, Louie is gone; his legacy is an upscale depanneur (convenience store).

gelato
Italian ice cream
parlour
British English spelling of parlor, a small shop

The trees still shudder. But there are few anglophones left. Most have left the area—some even the province—to find others in their language group. Québec is genuinely cordial. Canada is genuinely distant. It's just the way things are.

What More Did You Learn?

Discuss the following questions, based on the previous article, with a partner. Be prepared to explain your answers to the class.

1. Describe Outremont Avenue in your own words.
2. Who lived along Outremont Avenue in the 1950s?
3. What will the children do with ten cents?
4. Describe Robil's.
5. Why doesn't Carole Paradis play with the other children along her street?
6. What do the French and English children think of each other?
7. What has happened along Outremont Avenue since 1958?

Analyze It

Imagine that Carole Paradis has now grown up and is telling a friend from another culture about her childhood neighborhood. How do you think she would describe it. With a partner write a detailed dialogue of their conversation.

Tell Us More about It

Prepare an oral or written report on one of the following topics. Use the outline that follows to organize your presentation and take notes while researching.

Jacques Cartier   Paul de Chomedey
Samuel de Champlain   Huron nation
Expo '67   St. Lawrence River
Parti Quebecois   1976 Summer Olympic Games

Topic:

Major points to discuss about this topic:

1.

2.

3.

4.

Details to discuss about each major point:
Major Point 1

Major Point 2

Major Point 3

Major Point 4

9 | *Washington, D.C.*
"The Capital City"

Meeting at the Capitol Building

Predict!

Examine the pictures in this chapter. What do you already know about the politics and culture of Washington, D.C.? With a classmate, discuss how these pictures accurately or inaccurately represent what the city of Washington is about to your knowledge.

Vocabulary Preview

Choose the best definition for the underlined expression in each sentence. You will hear these phrases again when you listen to the recording about Washington.

a. moved from one place to another
b. referring to a narrow street or passage-way between or behind buildings
c. started
d. referring to differences between races of people

e. feelings from the inability to accomplish something properly
f. lived in
g. place
h. forced

___ 1. <u>Inhabited</u> by U.S. politicians and hundreds of foreign diplomats, Washington is well known as a center of international political activity.

___ 2. Jesuit priests from Maryland <u>established</u> religious missions along the Potomac River, near what is today the city of Washington.

___ 3. Northern and southern political leaders argued over the <u>site</u> for the new capital of the young country. New York City was selected initially, and then Philadelphia served as the capital.

___ 4. The national government was officially <u>transferred</u> there in 1800. The second president, John Adams, and his wife Abigail were the first occupants of the White House.

___ 5. The war <u>drove</u> many freed slaves and whites into the city, doubling its population.

___ 6. After the war, African Americans were briefly given the right to vote, but because officials were worried about <u>racial</u> problems, the Congress of the United States soon took away this right.

___ 7. There was a steady arrival of African Americans during the beginning of the twentieth century. With little housing available to them, the African Americans crowded into the city's <u>alleys</u>.

___ 8. Five years later, following the assassination of Martin Luther King, Jr., black <u>frustrations</u> led to violent riots in 1968.

What Do You Want to Know?

Compose two questions you would like answered by the time you finish this chapter about Washington, D.C. Present your questions to the class to see if anyone knows the answers.

Question 1.

Question 2.

Notetaking Strategy 9: Use a system of organization.

Make sure that your notes are organized in a way that you will be able to understand them later on when you will use them to study for an exam. Not only can you connect ideas with lines and arrows, as Notetaking Strategy 8 discussed, but you can also create an outline format so that you can group important information together. Here's an example from the lecture on Las Vegas:

    I. Gambling ⇨ Benjamin Siegel
       A. 1930s ⇨ arrived
       B. 1942 ⇨ started luxury casino
          1. Flamingo Hotel ⇨ finished 1946
          2. Las Vegas focused on glitter and gambling
       C. 1947 ⇨ shot in Calif.

Notetaking Exercise

What do these notes mean? First organize these notes on Phoenix, Arizona, in a way that is easy for you to understand, then construct complete sentences from the notes.

Egypt. legend
bird Phoen   every 500 years
A.D. 1450–   Hohok. Phoen.
farming   cotton
               weaving
disappeared—mystery   ruins
                 canals, artifacts, old culture

Are these good notes? Why or why not? What are good notes? Discuss this with a classmate.

The Main Points: First Listening

Listen to the recording once to understand only the main points.

What's the Point?
A. List the most important information contained in the lecture on Washington, D.C. Continue structuring your notes as you listen and write down new information.

I. Introduction

II. Early history

III. After American Revolution

Pierre L'Enfant

John Adams

IV. Civil War

V. 20th century

Great Depression

WWII

Today

Sights

B. Compare your notes with another classmate. Did you miss anything?

What Do You Remember?

A. From your notes, create two comprehension questions based on the main idea of the lecture on Washington, D.C.

Question 1.

Question 2.

B. Exchange questions with a classmate. Answer the questions your classmate created. Did you take enough notes to answer the questions?

Washington and the Capitol at night

Details, Details: Second Listening

A. Listen again for the details contained in the lecture on Washington, D.C. Use your notetaking outline to take complete notes, including as many details as you can write down.

B. Now, based on your complete notes, answer the following questions to help you better understand the details of the lecture.

1. Washington, D.C., is the .... most populated city in the country.

2. In 1608, ... explored the region that is today Washington.

3. The first capital of the United States was ....

4. The area that makes up Washington, D.C., includes land given up by

   .... and ....

5. According to Pierre L'Enfant, no building in Washington could be taller than

   ....

6. When it was still a new city, Washington was referred to as

   ....

7. In 1914, Congress passed ....

8. In the .... and ...., Washington was a center of

   activity for the anti–Vietnam War movement.

9. The largest museum in the United States is ....

10. Washington is the only major city in the United States to

    ....

Post-listening Activities

After listening twice, you're ready to examine information included in the lecture more closely.

What Really Happened?
Answer the following comprehension questions with a partner. Use your notes to help you discuss them fully.

1. Why was Washington an important city during the Civil War?

2. How was Washington, D.C., chosen as the nation's capital?

3. Who were the alley dwellers and what happened to them?

4. What happened in the city of Washington after the assassination of Martin Luther King, Jr.?

Talking about It

With a partner, plan a trip to Washington, D.C. You will spend a weekend there in late March. What kinds of things can you do?

Friday evening:
    Arrive at Washington National Airport at 4:00 P.M.

Saturday:
    Morning:

    Afternoon:

    Evening:

Sunday:
    Morning:

    Afternoon:

    Fly home at 7:00 P.M.

Vocabulary Blitz

Word Forms

Try to figure the correct form for each vocabulary word in the chart that follows. (Some words don't have different forms. Those are marked with Xs.)

Noun	Verb	Adjective	Adverb
	inhabit		XXXXXXXXXXX
	establish		XXXXXXXXXXX
site		XXXXXXXXXXX	XXXXXXXXXXX
	transfer		XXXXXXXXXXX
	drive		XXXXXXXXXXX
	XXXXXXXXXXX	racial	
	XXXXXXXXXXX	alley	XXXXXXXXXXX
frustration			

1. What are the _____ of New York called?
   a. inhabits
   b. inhabited
   c. inhabitants
2. The mayor announced the _____ of a new school.
   a. establish
   b. establishment
   c. established
3. Was the _____ to the new school a permanent one?
   a. transfer
   b. transferring
   c. transferred
4. The wild cats that the people _____ out of the neighborhood last week finally settled in the woods.
   a. drive
   b. drove
   c. driven
5. Some problems can be _____ motivated.
   a. race
   b. racial
   c. racially
6. Math _____ me.
   a. frustration
   b. frustrates
   c. frustrating

Vocabulary in Context

Check your definitions from the Vocabulary Preview. Fill in each blank with the appropriate word from the following list. Remember to change the form of the word when needed.

inhabit	establish	site	transfer
drive	racial	alley	frustration

1. Many different tribes of Native Americans originally _____ the area that is today the United States.

2. During the turbulence of the 1960s, many African Americans marched in protest of the increasing _____ violence in some parts of the country. Although not all tensions between different groups of people are resolved, people are living more peacefully today.

3. Many Native American tribes were _____ to extinction by the brutality inflicted upon them by European settlers in the New World. Today, you'll only find a few remaining Native American tribes in the United States.

4. _____ arose when the striking workers could not reach an agreement with the company's management over better working conditions. They felt as if the management were not treating them fairly.

5. I think this is a beautiful _____ for our new house. Let's build it here!

6. Many East Coast– and West Coast–based U.S. companies have _____ their headquarters in the central part of the United States, where costs are cheaper.

7. Mike was _____ from his company's headquarters in New York to their smaller office in Texas. He loves southern living now!

8. Many homeless people sleep in a city's _____, behind buildings, and in old abandoned structures for shelter.

Writing about It

Is Washington, D.C., similar to the capital of your country? Why or why not? Describe the most interesting things to do in the capital of your country. Try to use at least four of the vocabulary words learned in this chapter in your writing.

Read More about It

Read the following news article, then do the exercises that follow it.

New Memorial Pays Tribute to FDR

Associated Press, May 2, 1997, by Harry F. Rosenthal

A new national memorial took its place Friday beside those for Washington, Jefferson and Lincoln. In word and sculpture, it honors Franklin D. Roosevelt, who calmed a shaken nation, led it to victory in war and set in place a social system that still endures.

"We honor the greatest president of this great American century," said President Clinton, born after Roosevelt's death in 1945.

The memorial spreads over a 7.5-acre site between the Potomac River and the rim of the Tidal Basin with its cherry blossom walk. Its four open "rooms" depict Roosevelt's four terms in office—and the upheaval in the nation along with the toll it took on his health.

Roosevelt was the Democrat, the liberal, who set the standard for Democrats and liberals to follow. He was also the president who set conservatives' teeth on edge at the very mention of his name: To them he was "that man in the White House."

America still lives the Roosevelt legacy: Every time an elderly person cashes a Social Security check, each time a bank is rescued from failure, each time the Federal Reserve Board tinkers with the economy.

Under his direction, the government began its regulation of the airways, it provided unemployment insurance, set rules for labor-management disputes, established housing assistance.

In Roosevelt's time dozens of agencies, known by their alphabetical names, came into existence. Republicans called it socialism, but it stayed to bedevil them.

"He electrified the farms and hollows, but even more important, he electrified the nation, instilling confidence with every tilt of his head and boom of his laugh," said Clinton.

"It was that faith in his own extra-ordinary potential that enabled him to guide his country from a wheelchair, and from that wheelchair . . . he lifted a great people back to their feet and set America to march again toward its destiny."

For 52 years since FDR's death, the only monument to him in the capital was a stone block—the size of his desk—that stood in front of the National Archives. He wanted it that way.

On Friday, many of his grandchildren were in the audience. "It reminds me of the time when the entire American community pulled together," Christopher Roosevelt said of the monument. "A country's strength lies in its values and sense of community."

David Roosevelt, another grandson and a member of the memorial commission, said FDR's 12 years in office were "an era surpassed perhaps only by the Civil War in its infliction of pain and travail on the people of this nation."

He urged those who visit the memorial to use it to remember "the hopelessness and despair of those days from 1933 to 1945 and feel the qualities of a personality which gave hope and direction so a nation and its people could triumph."

One criticism of the memorial is that it fails to show FDR in the wheelchair he used after he was stricken with polio in 1921. Representatives of disabled groups were allotted a separate area in which to demonstrate.

Vice President Al Gore said in his tribute that one of the messages conveyed by the memorial "is that the greatest president of this century, who led this nation as no other could, was disabled."

That brought cheers from the many people in wheelchairs and crutches who watched the ceremony from an area immediately in front of the podium.

Afterward, when the memorial opened to the public, about a dozen people in wheelchairs held an impromptu news conference in front of a large statue of Roosevelt. When they left, a wheelchair and cane briefly remained behind as well as an aluminum walker.

Justin Dart, a lifelong advocate for the disabled, congratulated Clinton for asking Congress to add a sculpture depicting Roosevelt in a wheelchair.

"We celebrate. Yes, we congratulate," Dart said. "But for 42 years we've been planning this memorial and where is President Roosevelt in a wheelchair?"

The Lincoln Memorial in the foreground, backed up by the Washington Monument and the U.S. Capitol Building

Dart said he wants to see a major statue "that will dominate the images that go out from this memorial worldwide, that will send a message to every person in the world that this great leader founded the United Nations and defeated fascism in World War II from a wheelchair."

The dedication was held under cloudless skies before thousands of people. Clinton and other dignitaries—including the Netherlands' Princess Margriet, Roosevelt's goddaughter—had their speeches interrupted by noise from an unending stream of airplanes taking off from nearby National Airport.

Clinton and his wife, Hillary, later toured the memorial with its designer, landscape architect Lawrence Halprin, and made white putty impressions at one of the sculptures.

What More Did You Learn?

Discuss the following questions, based on the previous article, with a partner. Be prepared to explain your answers to the class.

1. What were some of the achievements of Franklin D. Roosevelt?
2. Describe the FDR Memorial.
3. Who referred to President Roosevelt as "that man in the White House"? Why?
4. According to President Clinton, what did President Roosevelt do for the country?
5. Why are some people critical of the memorial?
6. What does Justin Dart want?

Analyze It

What might the effects be on the American people of having a statue of President Roosevelt in a wheelchair? If you walked by the memorial and saw a statue like this of President Roosevelt, how would your image of him change? Discuss your thoughts with a partner and consider how disabled people are viewed in your country versus how they are viewed in the United States.

Tell Us More about It

Prepare an oral or a written report on one of the following topics. Use the outline that follows to organize your presentation and take notes while researching.

Potomac River	John Adams
Captain John Smith	American Civil War
Franklin Delano Roosevelt	Alley Dwelling Act
American Revolution	Martin Luther King, Jr.
George Washington	Smithsonian Institution
Pierre L'Enfant	Frederick Douglass

Topic:

Major points to discuss about this topic:

1.

2.

3.

4.

Details to discuss about each major point:
Major Point 1

Major Point 2

Major Point 3

Major Point 4

Side Trip

Colonial Williamsburg, Virginia

Photo by Mike Bell

Predict!

What do you know about Virginia? What do you know about early American settlements? With a partner, make a list of information you already know on this topic, including how these people lived and worked.

Key Expressions

Following are some expressions and names that might help you better understand the lecture on Colonial Williamsburg, Virginia:

Middle Plantation	Jamestown	Richmond	munitions
Rockefeller	embody		

Taking It All In

Listen to the mini-lecture twice. On your own piece of paper take notes of all the important information you hear. Then, mark each statement below with a T for true or an F for false, based on the notes you took. Be prepared to correct the false statements.

____ 1. Jamestown was the original name for Williamsburg.
____ 2. Williamsburg was made the capital of the state of Virginia in 1699.
____ 3. The College of William and Mary has existed in Williamsburg since 1695.
____ 4. The capital was moved to Richmond, Virginia, in 1780.
____ 5. John D. Rockefeller donated money so that Williamsburg, Virginia, could be made the capital once again.
____ 6. The people of Colonial Williamsburg wear costumes of the eighteenth century.
____ 7. These people tell stories about the seventeenth century.
____ 8. They also allow you to try your hand at their way of living.

Photo by Mike Bell

10 | *Chicago, Illinois*
"The Windy City" and "The City of Big Shoulders"

Predict!

Discuss the following questions with your classmates.

1. Look at the pictures throughout the chapter. What do you think Chicago has to offer to a resident and a visitor? Consider the environment and various scenery.
2. After looking at the pictures, why do you think Chicago has the two nicknames, "The Windy City" and "The City of Big Shoulders"?

Vocabulary Preview

From the list that follows, choose the meaning for each of the underlined expressions. You will hear these phrases again when you listen to the recording about Chicago.

a. the illegal sale of products
b. success, especially financial
c. design of buildings and other structures
d. organized as a legal town
e. feature in a landscape that is easily identifiable

f. agreement in feeling and opinion
g. located
h. work stoppage in an attempt to obtain more benefits from a company
i. starting from the beginning with nothing

____ 1. Situated on the shores of Lake Michigan on a relatively flat area of land, Chicago is today an international center for manufacturing, trade, and finance.

____ 2. Chicago, which had only forty-three houses and two hundred inhabitants, was incorporated as a village and by 1837 became a city.

____ 3. Surprisingly, the Civil War, the war that divided the southern and northern states, brought economic prosperity to the city.

____ 4. One of the few structures left standing was the three-year-old Gothic-style water tower on the north side of the city, which has become a favorite landmark for residents and visitors alike.

____ 5. The fire actually gave the people of Chicago a chance to plan their city from scratch.

____ 6. Hard economic times prompted many disputes by workers over the low wages offered by the factories. As a result, many workers went on strike to obtain higher salaries.

____ 7. Due to the illegality of alcohol, some people ventured into bootlegging and became rich.

____ 8. Today Chicago is known for its many blues clubs, but it is also known for its beautiful architecture and peaceful setting. Many of the buildings erected as a result of the Great Fire still stand.

____ 9. Although there have been problems between ethnic groups in the past, Chicago is promoting harmony among its people and is a welcoming city to visitors from near and far.

What Do You Want to Know?

Compose two questions you would like answered by the time you finish this chapter about Chicago, Illinois. Present your questions to the class to see if anyone knows the answers.

Question 1.

Question 2.

Notetaking Strategy 10: Omit unnecessary words.

Don't write down complete sentences. Omit words that are not necessary. Some common words you might omit are:

a, and, the, in, at, and forms of *have* and *be* as auxiliaries

Try to think of some other common words you might omit.

Notetaking Exercise

A. In the following paragraph, omit as many words as possible, while abbreviating as many of the remaining words as you can.

Because Chicago grew as a center for manufacturing, especially after the fire, many labor disputes resulted in the 1880s and early 1890s. What have become known as the Haymarket Riots occurred in May 1886 when a bomb was thrown into a labor meeting where participants were discussing the introduction of an eight-hour work day. Over one hundred fifty policemen had been called to quiet a reported riot there, but it turned deadly when seven policemen lost their lives. Later in the 1890s, hard economic times prompted many disputes by workers over the low wages offered by the factories. As a result, many workers went on strike to obtain higher salaries.

_____

_____

_____

_____

_____

_____

_____

_____

_____

_____

_____

B. Exchange your notes with a classmate. Review each other's notes for accuracy. How did you do?

The Main Points: First Listening

Listen to the recording once to understand only the main points.

A sightseeing cruise on the Chicago River

What's the Point?

A. List below the most important information contained in the lecture on Chicago, Illinois.

Introduction:

Explorers

19th century

20th century

B. Compare your notes with a classmate's notes. Did you miss anything?

What Do You Remember?

A. From your notes, create two comprehension questions based on the main idea of the lecture on Chicago, Illinois.

Question 1.

Question 2.

B. Exchange questions with a classmate. Answer the questions your classmate created. Did you take enough notes to answer the questions?

Details, Details: Second Listening

Listen again to comprehend some of the details about the lecture on Chicago, Illinois.

A. After listening once, make a list of the most important information in this lecture:

_____

_____

_____

_____

_____

_____

B. Compare your list with a classmate's list. Did you miss anything? Make note of anything you may have missed. Underline all the information you believe important in your original notes. Listen again and make note of any additional information to support what you've underlined.

C. Now, using your complete notes, answer whether the following statements are true or false. This will help you better understand the details of the lecture. Be prepared to correct the false statements.

____ 1. Chicago is located near Lake Ontario.
____ 2. Canadians Marquette and Jolliet were the first Europeans to explore the area that is today Chicago.
____ 3. The presence of Fort Dearborn attracted new settlers to what is today Chicago.

Sunbathing along Lake Michigan

___ 4. The United States Congress gave the Chicago community $25,000 to build a harbor.

___ 5. Abraham Lincoln was nominated for president at the Democratic National Convention, which was held in Chicago in 1860.

___ 6. One of the buildings that survived the Great Fire of 1861 was Chicago's Gothic Water Tower.

___ 7. Alcohol was illegal in Chicago during the 1920s.

___ 8. Al Capone was sent back to Italy by Johnny Torrio.

___ 9. In 1933 and 1934, Chicago hosted a successful World's Fair, the "Century of Progress Exposition."

___10. The Art Institute of Chicago has a collection valued at over $260 million dollars.

Post-listening Activities

After listening twice, you're ready to examine information included in the lecture more closely.

Putting the Pieces Together

Form four groups. Each group should only answer one of the following comprehension questions based on the lecture about Chicago. When your group has completely answered the question, one person from each of the four groups should join a different group. Present your answer to your new group. Be prepared to answer any possible questions.

Group 1
Describe the activities of the early settlers of Chicago.
Notes:

Group 2
Why is Chicago known as a convention city?
Notes:

Group 3
Describe the labor disputes that occurred in Chicago. What were they about?
Notes:

Group 4
Why are crime and corruption historically associated with Chicago?
Notes:

Talking about It
A good friend of yours is going to visit Chicago very soon. Tell him or her what you know about the city. With a partner, write a dialogue detailing this conversation.

Friend 1: _____

_____

Friend 2: _____

_____

Friend 1: _____

_____

Friend 2: _____

_____

Friend 1: _____

_____

Friend 2: _____

Vocabulary Blitz

Word Forms

Try to figure out the correct form for each vocabulary word in the chart that follows. (Some words don't have different forms. Those are marked with Xs.)

Noun	Verb	Adjective	Adverb
		situated	XXXXXXXXXXX
		incorporated	XXXXXXXXXXX
prosperity			
landmark	XXXXXXXXXXX	XXXXXXXXXXX	XXXXXXXXXXX
strike			XXXXXXXXXXX
bootlegging			XXXXXXXXXXX
architecture/			
harmony			

Now, choose the correct form for each word in parentheses in the following sentences.

1. Where did you _____ (situate) the garden at your new house?

2. The small village decided to _____ (incorporate) as a town.

3. Be well, and may all your dreams be _____ (prosper) ones.

4. The workers decided it was time for a _____ (strike).

5. That ivory statue is part of a _____ (bootleg) shipment that the government confiscated.

6. John decided to become an _____ (architecture).

7. It's wonderful when you have a _____ (harmony) relationship with someone.

Vocabulary in Context

Check your definitions from the Vocabulary Preview. Fill in each blank with the appropriate word from the following list. Remember to change the form of the word when needed.

situate	incorporate	prosperity	landmark	
from scratch	strike	bootlegging	architecture	harmony

1. The factory workers were angry that they were not receiving enough money, so they went on _____ .

2. The beautiful _____ of Paris is respected worldwide. The design of the Cathedral of Notre Dame is of special interest to many people.

3. Many criminals are trying to get rich from the _____ of cocaine.

4. The Taj Mahal is a _____ in Nepal known by people all around the world.

5. After the horrible riots in Los Angeles in 1992, the people of the city are now trying to create _____ among the different ethnic groups.

6. Although the city of Philadelphia was made up of many separate communities, it was finally _____ in the late eighteenth century.

The ruins of Chicago after the Great Chicago Fire, from the Nov. 4, 1871 issue of *Harper's Weekly*

7. The _____ of the wine industry in California allows wine makers to invest heavily in new and more efficient methods of making wine, leading to further success.

8. Do you know where the Water Tower is _____ in Chicago? I'd like to visit it.

9. Melissa made the cake _____ . She loves to cook and doesn't like the taste of cake made from cake mix.

Writing about What You've Learned

Chicago has been a center for stunning architecture since the rebuilding of the city after the Great Fire of 1871. What architectural landmarks define the character of your city? Explain how these structures are symbols of your city's personality. Try to use at least four of the vocabulary words learned in this chapter in your writing.

Read More about It

Read the following news article, then do the exercises that follow it.

Scorching Alteration:
The City's Face Was Never the Same after the Great Chicago Fire

Chicago Tribune, March 2, 1997, by Jane Adler

A hot, strong wind blew from the southwest. After a summer of little rain, the city was tinder dry.

In a **ramshackle** neighborhood of new immigrants, a barn caught fire. The wind drove the blaze to a nearby shed that contained two tons of coal and a large supply of kindling. The fueled flames jumped to a neighbor's fence and nearby rooftops. Trees burned. Airborne embers ignited the wood houses.

ramshackle
falling apart

So began, on Oct. 8, 1871, the Great Chicago Fire, a blaze that would engulf much of the city. In total, more than 17,000 buildings would be destroyed and 100,000 people left homeless. Some 300 died.

Real estate was, in many ways, a big part of the story. The wood buildings constructed before the fire were largely responsible for the rapid spread of the flames on that autumn evening, according to historians.

Barns and houses, sheds and factories were crowded together on small lots. The city was ready to burn.

The building boom after the fire also changed where most people would live. Fire codes were tightened, stipulating that buildings in the central business district be made of stone or brick. This accelerated the migration of residents toward the outer edges of the city where they could rebuild affordable wood houses.

"The thrust of public policy after the fire was to make the city fire-proof," said Henry Binford, associate professor of history at Northwestern University. "The net effect, though, was the decentralization of the city."

Before the fire, Chicago, like other developing frontier towns, was growing fast. With the promise of work, new immigrants and farm laborers flooded the city. Between 1850 and 1870, the population increased from 30,000 to 300,000. Houses were quickly built for new residents. Most were flimsy structures with one or two rooms.

"Chicago was an immigrant hub and the core of the city consisted mainly of shacks and shanties made of wood," said Victor Simmons, curator, Chicago Architecture Foundation.

Typical of many homes found in working-class Chicago neighborhoods was the O'Leary property on De Koven Street, site of the barn where the infamous fire allegedly began.

The lot was 25 by 100 feet. There were two small shingled buildings where the O'Learys and another family lived. Little space was left between the structures; they looked like one house. The property also had a coal shed and barn for a few farm animals. Despite modest circumstances, the O'Learys owned the property, which they'd bought for $500.

"Chicago was unusual at the time because a number of working-class people owned their homes and plots," said Karen Sawislak, assistant professor of history at Stanford University and author of the book, *Smoldering City*.

Because of the wind's direction the night of the fire, the O'Leary house miraculously wasn't destroyed. But others like it were. Most houses had a wood balloon frame, a construction method developed during the 1850s. Two-by-four studs were nailed together into a simple skeleton.

This time- and labor-saving technique, still used today, allowed new cities such as Chicago and San Francisco to grow quickly. But it also put residents at great risk of fire.

Fires were common in the mid-19th century. In 1868, there were 515 reported in Chicago. By October 1871, about six fires were breaking out every day. And on the night before the great fire, flames destroyed four city blocks.

Firefighting methods back then were inadequate for the growing number of people and buildings. Ill-equipped **brigades** found it hard to contain spreading flames.

brigades
organized groups

Of course, wealthy residents thought they had some measure of protection because their homes were made of stone and brick. But their homes had ornate wood interiors and were surrounded by wood stables, barns and small wood houses, putting those properties at risk, too.

Chicago homes weren't the only potential fire hazard. By some estimates, two-thirds of the city's 549,500 buildings, including commercial and public structures, were made of wood.

According to H.A. Musham, writing in a 1943 state historical paper, pre-fire buildings in the business district were three to five floors high. The tallest building was the new eight-story Palmer House. The exteriors of these relatively big buildings were only veneers of brick or stone.

The interiors hid wood frames and floors, topped with highly flammable tar or shingle roofs. Canvas and wood awnings were common. Fancy exterior decorations were carved from wood and then painted to look like stone or marble.

"It was a Victorian style with lots of ornamentation," noted Simmons of the Chicago Architecture Foundation.

Adding fuel to the fire, literally, were long stretches of wooden sidewalks and roads that criss-crossed the city.

Chicago had been founded on land that was low, flat and close to the water. As a result, elevated roadways and sidewalks had been constructed, mostly of wood, to lift the city out of the mud.

When the fire started, there were more than 600 miles of wooden sidewalks and 55 miles of pine block streets in the city, which now covered 23,000 acres.

The statistics in the fire's aftermath were sobering. The blaze burned more than 2,100 acres (about three-and-a-half square miles). Some 17,420 buildings were destroyed. Most of the 300 people who were killed lived in poor neighborhoods where cottages and shacks were doubled up on small lots.

Of note, the Chicago Water Tower is the only remaining landmark that survived the fire. The stone structure was isolated in the middle of a block. The wood interior did catch fire and was gutted, cutting off the city's water supply.

Just after the fire, reconstruction of the city began. Many of the new buildings and houses were similar to pre-fire structures, historians say. In most neighborhoods, little attention was paid to fire prevention.

The immediate need was housing. A relief committee was established to provide places for the poor, according to the book, *The Slum and the Ghetto*, by Thomas Philpott.

In the two years after the fire, the relief committee built four big frame barracks for the poor, and 8,000 small houses, also frame, for laborers.

Philpott says these emergency dwellings equaled the worst jerry-built huts destroyed in the fire, but they proved to be permanent. He says: "Dilapidated yet durable, they stood for decades." Several of these little houses, then deemed temporary, still exist in Chicago's Old Town neighborhood.

By the end of 1871, the city building commission reported the construction of more than 6,000 wooden shanties, 2,000 solid wood frame buildings and 500 structures of brick and stone.

While much of the city was being rebuilt in its former image, a dispute erupted over fire codes. The city fathers wanted to ban wood structures from the central district. But this meant a fair number of residents, still living close to the city center, could not afford to rebuild their homes with expensive brick or stone materials.

On Jan. 15, 1872, the German community staged a march to voice their anger over laws they felt were meant to penalize the poor. They thought the new fire laws would eliminate any possibility of their owning homes.

Even so, a year after the fire, an **ordinance** was enacted requiring that all new buildings in the city's core be made of non-combustible material. At the same time, land values were rising. The average lot shrank from 50 feet wide to about 25 feet wide by 125 feet deep, the size of the standard city lot today.

ordinance
regulation

The rebuilding of the city also attracted more new residents and laborers looking for housing. Generally, these workers had to live outside the fireproof belt, in wood houses or two-flats that were less expensive to build than the brick homes near the city's center.

"Most workers had little choice but to locate in the space between the fire limits and the outer zone of desirable suburbs," according to Philpott.

Downtown, the new commercial buildings were bigger and grander than their predecessors. The largest remaining collection of post-fire buildings currently sits at the northwest corner of Lake and Franklin streets. These four structures, built from 1872–75, provide a clue as to how the downtown appeared immediately following its reconstruction. The buildings include features like cast-iron columns and arched window openings.

The building boom was curtailed in 1873 by a national depression set off by a bank failure. And another devastating fire in July 1874 destroyed millions of dollars worth of post-fire structures. This caused the insurance industry to enforce a boundary for fire-proof structures, according to historian Sawislak.

As a result, the city tightened its fire ordinance. The circle within which wood structures were prohibited was widened and the decorative use of wood on buildings was prohibited.

Sawislak says newspaper advertisements from the period often featured wood homes for lower paid workers.

"Builders would advertise plots in the (North Side) Lakeview neighborhood that were outside the fire area," she said.

After six years, the depression lifted and another round of building began. The commercial building boom of the 1880s was spearheaded by famous architects such as Louis Sullivan and Daniel Burnham. This architecture was free of ornamentation and was more fire resistant.

In the 1880s, the world's first skyscrapers were being built in Chicago, using steel skeletons and newly invented elevators. It was the start of the renowned Chicago school of architecture.

More houses were built in the 1880s, too. According to Binford of Northwestern, construction methods were slowly changing, but true innovations, like plumbing and gas lines, were reserved for expensive homes. And despite its notorious history, wood still was the favored building material.

What More Did You Learn?

Discuss the following questions, based on the previous article, with a partner. Be prepared to explain your answers to the class.

1. Where did the fire start?
2. Why did it burn so quickly and spread so easily?
3. Explain why wealthy residents also weren't protected.
4. What were the dangers of the streets and sidewalks?
5. Why didn't the Water Tower burn?
6. What was the dispute over the fire codes about?
7. What stopped the building boom after the fire?
8. Describe the buildings of the 1880s in Chicago.

Looking up at the Sears Tower

Analyze It

Chicago had grown very quickly in the years leading up to the Great Fire in 1871. After the fire, the city government drew up a set of rules to prevent future catastrophic fires. With your group, discuss the rules probably drawn up by the city. Make a list and present them to the class, justifying each rule with an explanation of its purpose.

Tell Us More about It

Prepare an oral or a written report on one of the following topics. Use the outline that follows to organize your presentation and take notes while researching.

Lake Michigan	Columbian Exposition
Captain John Whistler	labor unions
Louis Jolliet	organized crime
Jacques Marquette	Prohibition
Abraham Lincoln	Al Capone
Great Chicago Fire	Art Institute of Chicago

Topic:

Major points to discuss about this topic:

1.

2.

3.

4.

Details to discuss about each major point:
Major Point 1

Major Point 2

Major Point 3

Major Point 4

11 | *Boston, Massachusetts*
"Beantown"

Predict!
Discuss the following questions with a class-mate.

1. Why do you think Boston is referred to as "Beantown"?
2. After examining the pictures throughout the chapter, how would you describe the city of Boston?

Vocabulary Preview
From the list that follows, choose the meaning for each of the underlined expressions. You will hear the first sentence in each pair again when you listen to the recording about Boston. The second sentence or set of sentences uses the same vocabulary in another context.

a. to gain the most power in a group
b. competition or fight to gain something
c. a descriptive or pet name used instead of the real name for a person, place, or thing
d. anger
e. prosperous

f. to move from place to place without a purpose
g. forced to receive a penalty for a crime or mistake
h. people who are the product of specific ancestors or family members

____1a. The Puritans had left England because they had been <u>punished</u> for expressing their religious beliefs. Ironically, the town leaders tried to <u>punish</u> anyone who did not share their same Puritan ideas.

1b. The little boy was <u>punished</u> by his mother for throwing food onto the floor.

____2a. Many Puritan women prepared baked beans every Saturday night and served them for Sunday dinner, which is what earned Boston the <u>nickname</u> "Beantown".

2b. Her name is Elizabeth, but everyone calls her Beth because that's her <u>nickname</u>.

____3a. Boston had become a <u>thriving</u> town, with a population of twelve thousand people from various political and religious backgrounds.

3b. My garden had been <u>thriving</u> until the drought came, then everything died.

____4a. In 1765, the colonies in America were in conflict with Great Britain, so colonists in Boston acted as the leaders in the <u>struggle</u> for independence.

4b. People need to work together in the difficult <u>struggle</u> against AIDS.

____5a. <u>Hostility</u> arose among native Bostonians who did not trust the Irish, prompting some of these Bostonians to put signs in the windows of their businesses that said, "No Irish Need Apply."

5b. I sense some <u>hostility</u> between the two of you. What's the matter?

6a. The <u>descendants</u> of the Irish immigrants began to <u>dominate</u> the political scene in Boston.

____6b. She claims to be a <u>descendant</u> of George Washington, but she has a different last name.

____6c. The Ottoman Empire <u>dominated</u> the western world for many centuries.

____7a. Boston's famous Freedom Trail allows visitors to <u>roam</u> the city on foot, bringing them to most of the historic spots in the downtown area.

7b. The cats <u>roamed</u> around the garden until they found something to eat.

What Do You Want to Know?

Compose two questions you would like answered by the time you finish this chapter about Boston, Massachusetts. Present your questions to the class to see if anyone knows the answers.

Question 1.

Question 2.

Notetaking Strategy 11: Highlight important information.
Underline or star examples of complicated or important information. When necessary, note examples of this information by using the abbreviations *ex* or *e.g.*, which mean "for example."

Notetaking Exercise

Read the following paragraph. Take notes on the information given. Star or underline important and complicated information. Note examples when necessary.

Washington's present population is the most educated in the United States, with twice as many college educated adults as the national average. The city has so many museums and art galleries that it is almost impossible to see everything they contain. The nation's largest museum, the Smithsonian Institution, is actually a group of museums that includes the Air and Space Museum and the National Zoo.

The city itself is probably the greatest work of art to be observed. Examples of almost every style and period of architecture exist in Washington. Some interesting buildings to view are the old Executive Office Building and the White House, and the most beautiful are the monuments to Presidents Thomas Jefferson, Abraham Lincoln, George Washington, and Franklin Delano Roosevelt.

_____
_____
_____
_____
_____
_____
_____
_____

The Main Points: First Listening

Listen to the recording once to understand only the main points.

What's the Point?
A. List the most important information contained in the lecture on Boston, Massachusetts.

Puritans:

British colonists:

19th century:

Major sights:

B. Compare your notes with a classmate's notes. Did you miss anything? If so, add it in your notes.

What Do You Remember?

A. From your notes, create two comprehension questions based on the main idea of the lecture on Boston, Massachusetts.

Question 1.

Question 2.

B. Exchange questions with a classmate. Answer the questions your classmate created. Did you take enough notes to answer the questions?

Details, Details: Second Listening

A. Read the following questions before you listen to the lecture again. Listen carefully for any information that relates to them. Fill in the information in your notes from the First Listening.

B. Then, after the second listening, answer the questions from the information in your notes.

1. Who were the original settlers of Boston? What happened to them?
2. Why did the Puritans leave England?
3. Describe the Puritans.
4. Describe the events surrounding the Boston Massacre.
5. What effect did immigration have on Boston?
6. What is Boston like today?

Post-listening Activities

After listening twice, you're ready to examine information included in the lecture more closely.

The romantic Swan Boats of the Boston Public Garden

What Happened When?
Put the following statements in chronological order by placing a number (1, 2, 3, etc.) next to each. Then, next to each statement, write the year in which the incident occurred.

____ The population of Boston was twelve thousand. Year_____
____ The Boston Massacre occurred. Year_____
____ A new system of highways was built around Boston. Year_____
____ Landfill projects doubled the physical size of Boston. Year_____
____ Boston became the capital of the Massachusetts Bay Colony. Year_____
____ James M. Curley first became mayor of the city. Year_____
____ The English Puritans founded the city of Boston. Year_____
____ The first subway system in the United States opened in Boston. Year_____
____ Wealthy merchants acted as the town leaders in Boston. Year_____
____ Irish immigrants arrived in the city. Year_____
____ The Boston Tea Party occurred. Year_____

What Really Happened?
A. Kenny has written a short paper about Boston for his history class but has gotten a lot of the facts wrong. Correct his errors so that he can get a better grade.

Boston, Massachusetts is located on the Pacific coast of the United States. It was

founded by Irish Puritans in 1630, who named the city after an old Native American tribe who used to live there. The Puritans were not very religious people. They accepted anyone who wanted to live among them, even if they had different beliefs. By the beginning of the eighteenth century, colonists in Boston found themselves in a war with Ireland. Many major battles occurred in the area, including the one known as the Boston Massacre. During the 1850s, many German emigrants came to Boston fleeing the tomato famine at home. Their presence caused a lot of tension between African Americans and whites in the city. This prompted some native Bostonians to put signs in their store windows reading, "No Whites Need Apply."

B. Now, using your notes, finish Kenny's report.

Vocabulary Blitz

Word Forms
Try to figure out the correct form for each vocabulary word in the chart that follows. (Some words don't have different forms. Those are marked with Xs.)

Noun	Verb	Adjective	Adverb
	punish		XXXXXXXXXXX
hostility	XXXXXXXXXXX		XXXXXXXXXXX
nickname		XXXXXXXXXXX	XXXXXXXXXXX
descendant		XXXXXXXXXXX	XXXXXXXXXXX
XXXXXXXXXXX		thriving	XXXXXXXXXXX
	dominate		
	struggle		XXXXXXXXXXX
XXXXXXXXXXX	roam	XXXXXXXXXXX	XXXXXXXXXXX

Now, choose the correct form for each sentence below.

1. Her father gave her a severe _____ .
    a. punish
    b. punishment
    c. punished
2. The wild cats approached us, showing their _____ .
    a. hostiles
    b. hostile
    c. hostility
3. My parents _____ me Buffy when I was three years old.
    a. nickname
    b. nicknamed
    c. nicknaming
4. My family _____ from royalty.
    a. descendant
    b. descend
    c. descends
5. Bob and Joyce are running a _____ business.
    a. thriving
    b. thrive
    c. thrived
6. The gene for brown eyes is _____ over the gene for blue eyes.
    a. dominant
    b. domination
    c. dominate
7. That was quite a _____ !
    a. struggle
    b. struggled
    c. struggling

Vocabulary in Context

Check your definitions from the Vocabulary Preview. Fill in each blank with the appropriate word from the following list. Remember to change the form of the word when needed.

punish	nickname	thriving	struggle	roam
	hostility	descendant	dominate	

1. In colonial America many criminals were _____ by being put on display in

    the town stockades for several days.

2. Early American pioneers _____ the country before finding an adequate place to settle and start a new life.

3. _____ arose between Native Americans and colonial settlers when the Native Americans felt threatened by the newcomers.

4. Many cities and states of the United States have _____ that reflect their identity and personality, such as New York being known as the "Empire State."

5. The Chicago Bulls _____ the basketball world in the 1990s, winning five championships in six years. Many doubt any other team will ever achieve this success.

6. The pioneer settlers of the New World _____ against nature and other elements before they were able to settle peacefully.

7. Since being successfully reintroduced to the area, the _____ moose population of Maine has caused some problems for residents there.

8. The *Mayflower,* which carried Puritan settlers, roamed off course and arrived in Plymouth, Massachusetts, instead of Virginia, in 1620. As a result, many of their _____ still live in the area today.

Writing about What You've Learned

Boston was founded by people representing the religious Christian sect of Puritanism. What is the strongest religion in your country, and how does it influence your life and the way your government is run? Try to use at least four of the vocabulary words learned in this chapter in your writing.

Read More about It

Read the following news article, then do the exercises that follow it.

Without Warning, Molasses in January Surged over Boston:
The Great Boston Molasses Flood

Smithsonian Magazine, November, 1983, by Edwards Park

When I was a boy in Boston and had reached a sufficiently sophisticated age, I was allowed to go downtown by myself. I was finally deemed capable of handling the ancient subway system and the narrow, clogged streets, and I responded by making ritualistic expeditions from the boring security of the Back Bay to the perilous excitements of Washington Street. This was my Gobi Desert, my Mountains of the Moon, my Tarzan Country.

My target was always Iver Johnson's, the famous old sporting-goods store that captured the hearts of Boston lads in those days. It faced on Washington Street near the edge of Scollay Square, that opening in the cow-path streets where stood the Old Howard, a **burlesque** theater famous for supplementing the curricula of Harvard students. "Always Something Doing, One to Eleven, at the Old Howard" read its ads in the *Boston Globe,* followed by the titillating phrase, "25 Beautiful Girls 25." Scollay Square was off limits to me, and no wonder.

But Iver Johnson's was a wholesome interest. There I could wander through aisles flanked by baseball bats; through thickets of split-bamboo fly rods and stubbles of short, steel bait-casting rods (fiber-glass rods and spinning reels were as yet unknown); through an arsenal of rifles and shotguns, blue steel barrels glinting against the warm-grained walnut stocks; and through a long array of woolen winter clothes and thick leather hunting boots. Boys were under the constant surveillance by supercilious clerks. I remember how surprised one of them was the day I actually bought something, but no matter. This was a place in which to build dreams.

Iver Johnson's displayed some of its own items in the window that overlooked Washington Street. Sleds shiny with varnish. Also, as I remember, a little .22 revolver. And bicycles. My two older brothers had both been given Iver Johnson bikes, and one of these fine old 28-inch wheelers was reposing in our basement, heavy with dust. It was supposed to be handed down to me, but there was now too much traffic in the Back Bay, even on Sunday mornings, for a kid to learn how to handle a big bike. I went without—and so learned to hate many aspects of modernity.

The way to reach Iver Johnson's was to take the subway to Park Street and walk northeast to a wonderful little byway called Cornhill, which

burlesque
type of theater that makes fun of people and events

pitched downward to Washington Street. You could smell Cornhill before you reached it because at its upper end was the Phoenix, a coffeehouse marked by the aroma of freshly ground beans. The rich scent filled the streets around and lured customers by the score.

Along with the coffee smell was another, equally pervading. One could discern throughout much of downtown Boston, and especially around the North End, the unmistakable aroma of molasses.

As a boy, I never questioned that odor, so strong on hot days, so far-reaching when the wind came out of the east. It was simply part of Boston, along with the swan boats in the Public Gardens and the tough kids swimming in the Frog Pond on the Common. But years later, when I was on the staff of the *Boston Globe,* I asked a colleague about it. We were walking over toward the North End, beyond Hanover Street, and our taste buds were guiding us toward one of the corner trattorias where North End Italians make, I swear, the world's finest pizza. I was thinking about the smell of pizza, and for once I was annoyed by that other smell—the Boston smell.

"Why does Boston smell of molasses?" I asked my friend.

He looked at me curiously. "Because of the molasses flood, of course," he said.

"Molasses flood?"

"Yeah. The thing we do special stories on every ten years. Haven't you worked on one yet?"

I admitted I had not. And then the little restaurant came into view and we entered and sat down to pizza and kitchen tumblers of cellar-made Italian wine. And I forgot molasses for a number of years.

My paper did short memory pieces about the Great Boston Molasses Flood on ten-year anniversaries of the event, which occurred in 1919. I didn't happen to work there in a year that had a nine at the end of it, and so remained largely ignorant about the original disaster. Older friends and relatives recalled it, but not very accurately, or in much detail. To learn more, I recently dug into the files of the *Globe* and pieced together fragile bits of brown newsprint as best I could . . .

Copp's Hill. It rises beside the conflux of the Charles River and Boston's inner harbor. It looks across at the yardarms of the USS *Constitution*— "Old Ironsides"—moored at the Boston Naval Shipyard over at Charlestown. A full-size American car trying to negotiate the side streets of Copp's Hill will probably park its whitewalls on both curbs. At the foot of the hill, at Salem Street, is the Old North Church where two lanterns were hung as a signal to Paul Revere, and in a little park next to the church is a statue of Revere himself. Old men sit by the statue on sunny days, playing checkers and arguing dramatically in Italian. Copp's Hill is right there in the North End, Boston's Little Italy.

Commercial Street. It loops around the salient of Copp's Hill from the Charlestown Bridge, east and south, to link with Atlantic Avenue. It rains with traffic—and it did so in 1919, but with different sounds. Instead of the thunder of today's diesels, there was the unmuffled blat of loaded lorries with solid rubber tires, the endless clop of work horses pulling freight wagons, and over all, the roar of the relatively new elevated railway—the "El"—that for years kept Commercial Street in its shadow.

On the water side of Commercial Street, opposite Copp's Hill, there stood in 1919 a giant storage tank. It had been built four years before by the Purity Distilling Company—massively constructed, with great curved steel sides and strong bottom plates set into a concrete base and pinned together with a stitching of rivets. It was built to hold molasses, that old Colonial commodity that stirs school day memories of the "triangle trade": slaves from Africa to the West Indies; molasses from the West Indies to New England; rum, made from the molasses, back across the Atlantic for a cargo of slaves. The old triangle had long been broken by 1919, but New England still made (and makes) rum, as well as baked beans, and the molasses for both still came (and comes) north from the Caribbean and New Orleans. In 1919, Boston's Purity tank could hold about two and a half million gallons of the stuff.

January 15, 1919. The weather had been mild for Boston—close to 40° F—and the streets were bare of snow. Two months before, the Great War (to end all wars) had ended, and the Yankee Division, the 26th, was coming home soon. That bloody adventure was over, and the nation was about to enter a great experiment—Prohibition. One more state needed to ratify the 18th Amendment, and a vote was scheduled the next day. With an eye perhaps to the future, Purity Distilling Company had sold out in 1917 to United States Industrial Alcohol. Thus that huge molasses tank, 50 feet tall and some 90 feet in diameter, could legally continue to supply alcohol to industry.

The big Boston tank was just about full. A ship from Puerto Rico had brought its contents up to about 2,300,000 gallons a few days before.

At noon on this January day, work around the molasses tank routinely slowed as laborers took time out for their sandwiches and coffee. Men paused to eat and chat in a shack owned by the Paving Department, which shared the open area where the tank stood. Others were doing the same at the quarters of a Boston Fire Department fireboat on the waterfront side of the tank.

They were most probably discussing baseball—Boston had won the World Series in 1918—and a new film called *Shoulder Arms* which was Charlie Chaplin's satire on life in the trenches. They probably mentioned politics, for President Wilson was in Europe trying to get a peace treaty based on his Fourteen Points. Moreover, Theodore Roosevelt had died only two weeks before, and like him or not, you had to admire the man, even if you were a Boston day laborer.

They would certainly have been hashing over Boston's own politics, ever a fascinating subject. Ex-Mayor John J. Fitzgerald was by now out of the picture and these workmen probably said, "more's the pity," for "Honey-Fitz" never lost sight of his Irishness and seemed a darlin' man to the workers, despite stories of **graft**. One of his grandsons—the one named for him: John Fitzgerald Kennedy would be two years old in May. Fitzgerald himself had been born in the North End back when it was Irish and not yet Italian.

graft
money or influence gained in an illegal way

And certainly the flu epidemic would have been on the tongues of these workers. It took some 20 million lives around the world, more than half a million in the United States. There was nothing a man could do about it, it seemed, except go regularly to church and burn a few candles. But these men needn't have worried about the flu that day, for their own particular disaster was on the way.

At about 12:30, with a sound described as a sort of muffled roar, the giant molasses tank came apart. It seemed to rise and then split, the rivets popping in a way that reminded many ex-soldiers of machine-gun fire. And then a wet, brown hell broke loose, flooding downtown Boston.

Spill a jar of kitchen molasses. Then imagine an estimated 14,000 tons of the thick, sticky fluid running wild. It left the ruptured tank in a choking brown wave, fifteen feet high, wiping out everything that stood in its way. One steel section of the tank was hurled across Commercial Street, neatly knocking out one of the uprights supporting the El. An approaching train screeched to a stop just as the track ahead sagged into the onrushing molasses.

When the molasses wave hit houses, they "seemed to cringe up as though they were made of pasteboard," wrote one reporter. The Clougherty home at the foot of Copp's Hill collapsed around poor Bridget Clougherty, killing her instantly. And when pieces of the tank hit a structure, they had the effect of shellfire. One jagged chunk smashed the freight house where some of the lunchers had been working.

The great brown wave caught and killed most of the nearby laborers. The fireboat company quarters was splintered. A lorry was blasted right through a wooden fence, and a wagon driver was found later, dead and frozen in his last attitude like a figure from the ashes of Pompeii.

How fast is molasses in January? That day the wave moved at an estimated 35 miles an hour. It caught young children on their way home from the morning session of school. One of them, Anthony di Stasio, walking homeward with his sisters from the Michelangelo School, was picked up by the wave and carried, tumbling on its crest, almost as though he were surfing. Then he grounded and the molasses rolled him like a pebble as the wave diminished. He heard his mother call his name and couldn't answer, his throat so clogged with the smothering goo. He passed out, then opened his eyes to find 3 of his sisters staring at him. (Another sister had been killed.) They had found little Anthony stretched under a sheet on the "dead" side of the body-littered floor.

The death toll kept rising, day after day. Two bodies showed up four days after the tank burst. They were so battered and glazed over by the molasses that identification was difficult. The final count was 21 dead, 150 injured, a number of horses killed. The molasses wave, after spreading out, covered several blocks of downtown Boston to a depth of two or three feet. Although rescue equipment was quick to arrive on the scene, vehicles and rescue workers on foot could barely get through the clinging muck that filled the streets.

A news reporter later remembered seeing Red Cross volunteers, Boston debutantes in smart gray uniforms with spotless white shirtwaists and shiny black **puttees**, step determinedly into the deep brown muck. In seconds they were gooey and **bedraggled**, plunging through the flood that sucked at their puttees.

puttees
coverings of the legs
from ankle to knee

bedraggled
messy

Apparently one reason the ambulances arrived so soon was that a policeman was at his corner signal box, making a call to his precinct, when he glanced down the street and saw the brown tide slithering toward him. You can hear in your mind his gasp into the phone: "Holy Mother iv God! Sind iverythin' ye can—somethin' tirrible has happened!"

Most of the facts about the Great Molasses Flood emerged in the findings of the lawsuits that swamped Boston after the event and were just as sticky as the molasses. Litigation took six years, involved some 3,000 witnesses and so many lawyers that the courtroom couldn't hold them all.

The reason for the lawsuits was disagreement as to the nature of the disaster. What in the world had caused it? Three explanations arose: there had been an explosion inside the tank (in which case the fermentation of the molasses would be to blame); there had been a bomb set off (not so wild a possibility in those early days of Bolshevism—bombs had already blasted a few American industrial plants); there had been a structural failure of the four-year-old tank (which made United States Industrial Alcohol liable).

Eventually the court found that the tank had simply ruptured because the "factor of safety" was too low. In other words, inspections hadn't been tough enough. The company was held to blame for the horror. Settlements of more than 100 claims were made out of court. Industrial Alcohol paid off between $500,000 and $1,000,000. Survivors of those killed reportedly got about $7,000 per victim.

Molasses is the main by-product of the manufacture of sugar from sugar cane. It results from the continued boiling of the cane juice—reminiscent of the boiling off of maple sap to produce maple syrup. When enough re-boiling has gone on to wrench every bit of sugar out of the molasses, the resulting viscous liquid is blackstrap, the extra-thick molasses used as an additive in cattle feed. It provides valuable carbohydrates in the diet of a cow. (In ours, too, it seems. Recently, molasses has excited natural-food addicts as a sugar substitute.)

Back in 1919 you couldn't have given the product away in Boston. The gluey chaos caused by the flood was cleaned up by hosing the area with salt water from fireboats and then covering the streets with sand. The trouble was that all the rescue workers, clean-up crews and sightseers, squelching through the molasses, managed to distribute it all over Greater Boston. Boots and clothing carried it into the suburbs. Molasses coated streetcar seats and public telephones. Everything a Bostonian touched was sticky. There is a report that molasses even got as far as Worcester. Certainly the inner harbor turned brown as the hoses washed the goo into the bay.

As the rescue workers and clean-up crews tackled the incredible mess the night of January 16, they paused in puzzlement at the sudden ringing of church bells all over downtown Boston. Nebraska had voted on the 18th Amendment and ratified it. Prohibition was law, and churches which had campaigned for it in their pulpits now celebrated. Men up to their ankles in the makings of rum listened for a moment and went back to work.

The smell of molasses remained for decades a distinctive, unmistakable atmosphere of Boston. My boyhood association of the sweet aroma, mingled with the fragrance of coffee from the Phoenix, led me into a habit I still enjoy, though most other people seem to shun it: I invariably sweeten my first cup of early morning coffee with a teaspoonful of dark molasses. To me, the two go together.

But the Phoenix coffeehouse did not prove as permanent as the morning ritual it inspired. It was sacrificed to the great rebuilding of the inner city which took place mostly in the 1960s, and, unlike its namesake, it has not risen again. Even Cornhill has gone. Even the Old Howard. Even Iver Johnson's. And finally, even the smell of molasses. I passed the site of the catastrophe recently and found out there is little to show for it. Copps Hill is the same as ever, but the El is gone, and the old waterfront, once so messy with decrepit warehouses, has been largely redesigned and landscaped. Where the great doomed tank once stood, there is a park filled with swings, slides and the shouts of children, and next to it, an enclosed recreation center.

A retrospective account of the flood indicated that the "high molasses mark" could still be seen on walls and buildings in the area. I looked and saw a dark stain—but it was just a city stain with nothing to indicate that the gush of molasses had lapped that high and painted the stone brown. I couldn't even find a plaque, not the merest marker to remember the 15th of January, 1919. I sniffed the dark stain. Nothing.

But as I get older, early impressions express themselves suddenly and in strange ways. And as everyone knows, nothing is more nostalgic than a smell or a taste. One morning, not long before I started looking into the story of the flood, I was drinking my early coffee, hot and delicious, with just that faint touch of molasses to give it special meaning. And inexplicably I said, "I wish I had a bicycle."

"What on Earth for?" my wife asked me.

"I don't really know, come to think of it," I answered.

What More Did You Learn?

Discuss the following questions, based on the previous article, with a partner. Be prepared to explain your answers to the class.

1. How did the author come to learn of the Molasses Flood?
2. Why did Boston need so much molasses?
3. What was the molasses in the big tank to be used for on that day in 1919?
4. What were people doing around noon on January 15, 1919?

The colonial era Fanueil Hall is overshadowed by a modern Boston skyscraper

5. Who were the victims of the molasses flood?
6. Why was the rescue effort hampered?
7. Discuss the litigation that resulted from the Molasses Flood.
8. What was the court ruling that resulted from the litigation?
9. What did the ringing of the church bells signify?

Analyze It

With a group analyze how you might have felt had you witnessed this accident. Write a short newspaper article reporting what you saw.

Tell Us More about It

Prepare an oral or a written report on one of the following topics. Use the outline that follows to organize your presentation and take notes while researching.

Shawmut tribe of Native Americans
Puritans
Boston Massacre
American Revolution
Irish in Boston

John J. Fitzgerald
James M. Curley
Boston Common
Boston Symphony Orchestra
education in Boston

Topic:

Major points to discuss about this topic:

1.

2.

3.

4.

Details to discuss about each major point:
Major Point 1

Major Point 2

Major Point 3

Major Point 4

12 | *New York, New York*
"The Big Apple"
and "The City that Never Sleeps"

Predict!

Examine the pictures throughout the chapter, then discuss the following questions with a classmate.

1. How large do you think New York is in physical size and in population?
2. What do you already know about New York City? What more do the pictures tell you?

Vocabulary Preview

From the list that follows, choose the best meaning for each of the underlined expressions. You will hear these phrases again when you listen to the lecture about New York City.

___ 1. The Dutch company made many more <u>expeditions</u> to the area over the next ten years, leading to the establishment of the first permanent settlement.
   a. trips with a purpose
   b. quickness
   c. agreements

____ 2. Because the government of New Amsterdam was <u>tolerant</u> of religious freedom and of different immigrant populations, people from all over Europe decided to settle there.
a. unwilling
b. believing
c. accepting

____ 3. Minuit purchased the island of Manhattan from the Carnarsees for a number of small tools and <u>trinkets</u>.
a. small pieces of jewelry
b. money
c. land that they wanted to trade

____ 4. The British decided to make New York their <u>headquarters</u> in North America because it was centrally located between Massachusetts and Virginia.
a. a place for horses
b. center of an organization
c. bedroom

____ 5. The <u>inauguration</u> of General George Washington as the first president took place on the balcony of Federal Hall.
a. election
b. special ceremony to initiate someone into a new job
c. special treatment by his soldiers

____ 6. The largest <u>concentration</u> of African Americans was found in Harlem, to which African Americans began to move in 1905.
a. center of an organization
b. thinking hard
c. large group in a small area

____ 7. Although <u>technically</u> still part of New York City, by 1930 Harlem was known as the largest "black city" in the world.
a. not really
b. scientifically
c. actually

____ 8. Classical music is also very <u>prominent</u> in New York City.
a. popular
b. often
c. unpopular

What Do You Already Know?
With a partner list three things you know about New York today.

_____

_____

_____

Notetaking Strategy 12: Leave room for missed information.
Leave blank spaces for items or ideas you might miss. Often, the lecturer will say a lot of important information in a short period of time, making it difficult for the listener to write down everything. After the lecture, compare your notes with another student's and fill in your missing information.

The Main Points: First Listening

Listen to the recording once to understand only the main points.

What's the Point?
Take notes in the following outline. After you listen to the lecture once, compare your notes with another student's. How much of the most important information did you miss?

I. Intro

II. 16th–17th centuries

18th century

19th century

20th century

What Do You Remember?

A. From your notes, create two comprehension questions based on the main idea of the lecture on New York, New York.

Question 1.

Question 2.

B. Exchange questions with a classmate. Answer the questions your classmate created. Did you take enough notes to answer the questions?

Details, Details: Second Listening

A. Listen again to comprehend some of the details about New York, New York. Fill in the information you missed the first time in your notes.

B. Now, using your complete notes, fill in each blank with the missing information.

1. Today, New York has a population of ....

2. The area of New York City was first explored by ....

.... and later by ....

3. In 1625, the Dutch West India Company sent .... to hold

....

4. In ...., the British took control of New York.

5. New York was an established commercial center by the time of

....

6. The inauguration of

....

as ....

took place on the balcony of

....

7. By ....,

.... was known

as the largest "black city" in the world.

8. By 1980, twenty percent of New York City's population was

....

9. ....

is one of the great music halls in the world.

Post-listening Activities

After listening twice, you're ready to examine information included in the lecture more closely.

Putting the Pieces Together
Form four groups. Each group should only answer one of the following comprehension questions based on the lecture about New York. When your group has completely answered the question, one person from each of the four groups should join a different group. Present your answer to your new group. Be prepared to answer any possible questions.

Group 1
Who were the Native Americans that lived in the area that is today New York? What happened to them?
Notes:

Group 2
Describe the British presence in New York.
Notes:

Group 3
What happened in the 1840s, and how did it affect the growth of the city of New York?
Notes:

Group 4
Describe the presence of the African American population in New York City.
Notes:

What Really Happened?

Pretend that you are a Dutch settler living in New Amsterdam in 1664. With a partner write a dialogue in which you discuss the events that have occurred since you have arrived in the community.

A:

B:

A:

B:

A:

B:

A:

B:

A:

B:

Vocabulary Blitz

Word Forms

Try to figure out the correct form for each vocabulary word in the chart that follows. (Some words don't have different forms. Those are marked with Xs.)

Noun	Verb	Adjective	Adverb
expedition	XXXXXXXXXXXX		XXXXXXXXXXXX
		tolerant	
trinket	XXXXXXXXXXXX	XXXXXXXXXXXX	XXXXXXXXXXXX
headquarters		XXXXXXXXXXXX	XXXXXXXXXXXX
inauguration			XXXXXXXXXXXX
concentration			XXXXXXXXXXXX
XXXXXXXXXXXX	XXXXXXXXXXXX	XXXXXXXXXXXX	technically
	XXXXXXXXXXXX	prominent	

Now, fill in each of the following sentences with the correct word form.

1. Where will you go on the _____? (expedition)

2. I can't _____ much more noise from them. (tolerant)

3. Where will they _____ the new company? (headquarters)

4. I went to the _____ ball. (inauguration)

5. There is a large _____ of cats at the beach. (concentration)

6. He rose to _____ as he was elected to each new office. (prominent)

Vocabulary in Context
Check your definitions from the Vocabulary Preview. Fill in each blank with the appropriate word from the following list. Remember to change the form of the word when needed.

expedition	tolerant	trinkets	headquarters
inauguration	concentration	technically	prominent

1. Even though I do not like to smoke, I am _____ of him smoking cigarettes.

2. The _____ of the United Nations is located in New York.

3. There is a large _____ of children in our neighborhood but not very many elsewhere in town.

4. George Washington, the first president of the United States, is a _____ figure in American history.

5. We planned a shopping _____ for next week. We both needed a lot of new clothes for our trip to Hungary.

6. Eli wasn't rich, but he did have a few _____ left in his fire-damaged home.

7. The _____ of the president of the United States occurs every four years on January 20, at twelve noon exactly.

8. I am _____ a member of the English Club, but I never attend any of the meetings.

Writing about What You've Learned

The original settlers of New York City were Native Americans. They were pushed out by the European settlers and eventually died off. In the history of your country, have there been groups of people that have been pushed out? Who are they and what has happened to them? Try to use at least four of the vocabulary words learned in this chapter in your writing.

Read More about It

Read the following news article, then do the exercises that follow it.

Reluctant Welcome:
They Stepped off the Boat onto Ellis Island, to Hostile Glares, Discrimination and Blame. In 100 Years, Not Much Has Changed.

Los Angeles Times, October 3, 1993, by Josh Getlin

When it comes to immigrants, the mood is getting ugly.

Jobs are scarce and as the U.S. economy sputters, people accuse foreigners of stealing paychecks from Americans. One huge labor union poster says it all: "Restrict All Immigration. Protect Yourself And Your Children Against Ruinous Labor And Business Competition Through Unrestricted Immigration."

Millions talk wistfully about the good old days, when immigrants seemed less exotic, more respectful and truly eager to learn the English language. Anger is heating to a fever pitch in California, where citizens groups are lobbying for a crackdown on further immigration.

Meanwhile, politicians vow to seal U.S. borders and halt the flood of newcomers. The backlash boils into the press, where cartoons and commentaries inflame passions.

"Spoiling the Broth!" says a *Los Angeles Times* cartoon, ridiculing the "teeming millions" pouring into the American melting pot, as Uncle Sam looks on helplessly. "The U.S. Hotel Badly Needs a Bouncer!" shouts another newspaper's broadside.

Immigration 1993?

Try 1885 through 1921, a time when newcomers bore the hostility of a nation's economic turmoil—just like today. The Statue of Liberty may welcome the wretched refuse of someone else's teeming shore, but Americans have traditionally given newcomers the cold shoulder when times get tough, blaming them for everything from rising crime to declining morals.

"That's the downside of our great national self-image," says David Riemers, a New York University history professor and immigration expert. "We love to get misty-eyed about our open-door policies. But we're also pretty nasty to newcomers when it suits our needs."

Few places reflect this recurring American contradiction better than Ellis Island, the historic gateway for 12 million U.S. immigrants from 1892 to 1954.

The former munitions depot in New York harbor was once the nation's main port of entry, and a symbol of welcome rivaling the Statue of Liberty. Over the years, it has exerted a powerful grip on America's conscience, exemplifying a spirit of generosity and tolerance.

Yet that rosy picture has long been tempered by hard political realities. Those who came through Ellis Island battled prejudice, and today's anger over immigration echoes their struggles.

It's been a family fight: Nearly 100 million people—or about 40% of the nation's population—can trace their lineage to the Ellis Island pioneers. Russians. Italians. Irish. West Indians. Poles. Scandinavians. All braved rough seas, rotten food and cramped **steerage** compartments of aging steamships to reach America and start over. Once they did, some never let them forget they were different.

steerage
least expensive
passenger section of a
ship

"With immigration, everything runs in cycles," says Marian Casey, an author who is writing a history of the Irish in New York City. "The same fights recur over and over, and it really doesn't matter which group you're talking about. It's always been push and pull."

To be sure, there are differences: Those who came through Ellis Island were carefully monitored, given medical checkups and turned away if they failed to meet federal standards. Many quickly learned English, blended in and found work. Few sought public assistance. But that didn't spare them the ridicule of their new neighbors, who gawked as they walked down the gangplanks.

Boat people still come to Ellis Island—but only as tourists. After years of neglect, the old complex re-opened in 1990 as a Museum of Immigration. It's uplifting, yet paradoxical: While exhibits promote diversity, they clash with the current mood of immigrant-bashing. Indeed, some experts say the island's feel-good glow may be outdated.

"How do you square the images of this place with the reality of immigration issues today?" asks Thomas Kessner, an author and history professor at City University of New York. "Lots of folks say we have to shut the door now. Others disagree pretty strongly."

The debate has flared for more than 100 years, and it continues on a recent morning as a ferry leaves Manhattan and chugs toward Ellis Island. Once again, a ship of strangers sails past the Statue of Liberty and deposits them in front of the old way station. Their views on immigration are as varied as the countries from which their ancestors first came.

"There it is! My god, there it is!" exclaims Nancy Lieggi, as the quiet brick fortress of Ellis Island rises out of an early-morning mist. "I've waited forever to see this place!"

Lieggi, a Spanish teacher at Chatsworth High School in Canoga Park, grabs a companion's elbow and excitedly points out the island. She gestures at the Statue of Liberty. Soon, curious onlookers gather as she retraces an epic immigrant journey.

"My grandfather came from Southern Italy to Ellis Island, and that's how our family made it to America in the first place," Lieggi says, bursting with pride. "Now I'm walking the same route he did. The only thing missing is that I should be wearing a babushka!"

A small, bubbly woman in her 40s, Lieggi adjusts her hair in the absence of the Russian kerchief she's described and she grows impatient. There's no time to wait, she tells her slower companions, dragging them up the stairs into the museum. They can eat lunch later.

"I wish everybody could come to Ellis Island, because Americans tend to forget that we were all strangers here at one point," Lieggi says. "There's a lot of anger toward immigrants in California these days. But I think a lot of that stems from a lack of respect."

Jobs are a key issue, she concedes, because people are afraid of losing out to Central Americans or Asians: "But we're the lucky ones. We're here. And so maybe we shouldn't be so quick to shut the door. If we had, would my grandfather have ever made it to America?"

Back on the boat, others are less upbeat. Gary Bresson, a salesman in his 50s from Florida, notes proudly that his Russian-Jewish grandparents came through Ellis Island around 1900. They had to fight for everything, he says. Today's immigrants pose different problems.

"There's a mean spirit in America today over these people," Bresson suggests. "And part of it is that we've got to control our borders and enforce our laws. We can't be a sponge anymore and absorb everybody. Frankly, I don't know if America has room for any more people."

Across the deck, Cindalea Edwards nods approvingly. She lives in Oregon but grew up in Glendale, and she's familiar with California's concerns over illegal immigrants. She's also heard about Gov. Pete Wilson's plans to deny health and education benefits to illegals.

"No question, we have to reduce the number of people flooding into California. It's out of control," Edwards notes. "But the anger these days seems greater than I remember. It's almost as if people were at the breaking point."

As a companion smiles in agreement, Edwards suddenly looks guilty and shakes her head. "What I just said sounds kind of rough, and I guess it is," she confesses. "I don't know how you'd seal off the Mexican border, or if that's even what we want to do. When I think of this island, I'm reminded that we're supposed to be better people than that."

Are we? For those unsure, the museum offers an eye-opening course in U.S. racial and ethnic history. It hits them in the face the minute they enter the building.

Of those immigrants who came to the Americas, for example, nearly 6 million were African slaves, according to one exhibit. The conquering white men also stirred up trouble for their hosts: Native Americans declined from 5 million in 1500 to fewer than 250,000 in 1900.

Asians surpassed Spanish-speaking people in the 1980s as the largest group coming to the U.S., according to a chart. More than 5 million immigrants came from 1980 to '90, a huge total compared to earlier years. Seven million will immigrate between 1990 and 2000, not counting those here illegally. Currently, the U.S. admits about 800,000 immigrants legally each year.

"How can we permit this?" asks Jake Reinhold, a New Jersey trucker who has taken the day off to visit Ellis Island with his family. "Look at these figures about the Mexicans. I got the solution. I really do. Just put 'em back on the boat, baby. Outta here."

Reinhold's sentiments are provocative, even outrageous. They're also nothing new in the American experience. All he has to do is wander upstairs to the exhibit on immigration's history, and he'll find a roomful of kindred spirits from the 19th and 20th centuries.

To get there, he'll have to make his way past exhibits where visitors mass in front of computerized television screens and trace their own families' immigrant paths. He'll have to fight his way by uplifting stories of courage and **grit**, and the Wall of Honor, which proudly lists the names of some of the people who made the long journey to America. For the most part, Ellis Island tells an upbeat tale.

grit
courage with a positive attitude

But Reinhold won't have any trouble finding the darker side.

America absorbed more than 24 million immigrants at Ellis Island and other ports from 1880 to 1924, a staggering number compared to previous decades. The numbers swelled even as the U.S. economy bogged down in an 1893 recession, throwing thousands out of work. By 1910, 75% of the residents of New York, Boston and Chicago were immigrants or children of immigrants. Many Americans were not pleased.

Ellis Island highlights that hostility, and parallels with today's climate are sobering. The 1885 labor poster calling for Americans to "Restrict All Immigration . . ." takes an entire wall, and an adjoining room features the militant lyrics of a 1923 song:

> O Close the Gates of our nation, lock them firm and strong
> Before this mob from Europe shall drag our color down
> There are Places here already, our flag is forbidden to wave
> O! Close the gates of our nation, our liberty to save.

As visitors filter through the room, some shake their heads with disgust. "It's amazing that people were so worried about Europeans," says Evelyn Baker, an elderly Bay Area tourist. "They turned out to be good Americans. They had a right to be here."

Baker moves on and groans at the 1923 photo of a Hollywood home-owner on her porch, with a banner reading: "Japs keep moving. This is a White Man's neighborhood." It was all part of a "Swat the Jap" campaign that swept California long before World War II, and a companion pamphlet read: "We don't want you with us, so get busy, Japs, and get out of Hollywood."

Baker looks appalled. Then she changes her tune. California has too many people now, she says flatly. And the latest arrivals are, well, different. "I never thought I'd be in favor of clamping down on immigration, but I am," she says. "In California right now they're walking across the border. And look at these gang members. Their parents just don't care what the children do. We have to control our borders."

It's an old refrain.

In 1882, Congress banned Chinese, along with "any convict, lunatic, idiot or any person unable to take care of himself without becoming a public charge." In 1903, the regulations expanded to exclude epileptics, professional beggars and anarchists.

Americans have long supported the idea of immigration. They only have trouble with the latest newcomers, whomever they happen to be. Like the Irish, who arrived in droves after 1840.

"The Irish were considered not merely foreigners, but an unassimilable group," historian Thomas Sowell wrote in *Ethnic America*. "In an argument destined to be repeated about many groups, it was claimed that, although earlier immigrants could be absorbed into the mainstream of American life, the peculiar characteristics of this group made that impossible."

Unless, of course, there was work to be done. Just ask the businessmen who have made a fortune off immigrants. One of the museum's most vivid posters is an 1885 ad for the Central Pacific Railroad: "California: Cornucopia of the World. Room for Millions of Immigrants! Railroad and private land for a million farmers. A climate for health and wealth!"

San Francisco boosters sent out a call for immigrant laborers to help rebuild the city after the 1906 earthquake. The Brooklyn Bridge could never have been finished without thousands of construction workers from Italy and other countries. Yet even these immigrant achievements weren't enough to assuage those who felt threatened by newcomers.

The real crackdown began in 1921, when lawmakers cut the annual immigration ceiling to 350,000 and quotas limited arrivals from "problem regions" like southern and eastern Europe. In 1924, the ceiling was again lowered, to 150,000. Those limits remained in effect until 1965, when Congress opened the doors to millions of new arrivals. A 1986 law had a similar impact, granting amnesty to millions who had been living illegally in the United States. By 1990, Congress had repealed earlier laws excluding various types of people or entire ethnic groups.

"We have a **see-saw** pattern in America when it comes to immigration, and people don't remember that," says Ed O'Donnell, a tour director leading a group of teachers through the Ellis Island museum. "We say that immigrants made us strong, but we give them a rough time."

see-saw
up and down

As he speaks, O'Donnell guides his group past an exhibit of Tin Pan Alley sheet music from the early 1900s that ridiculed immigrants and mocked their old-world customs. The titles would be considered racist today, but they once entertained millions: "I'm Going Back to the Land of Spaghetti," "In Blinky Winky Chinky Chinatown," and "Yonkle the Cowboy Jew."

His biggest job, O'Donnell says, is reminding people to keep an open mind.

That's easier said than done.

As the group files past the music exhibit, one teacher speaks for her colleagues when she asks about a solution: Do we just let everyone into this country?

"We need to find common ground," O'Donnell suggests. "You have people who want to seal off the Mexican border with troops, and that's not going to happen. But maybe we should expect that newcomers will learn our language, and that our immigration laws will be enforced."

By mid-afternoon, most boat people have had their fill of Ellis Island and they slowly crowd back onto the Manhattan-bound ferry.

"I recently had some tourists say that the problem with today's immigrants is that they're so bizarre and unpredictable," says O'Donnell, watching the large hall empty. "And I remind them there was nothing stranger to an American in 1906 than the sight of an Orthodox Jew walking down the street. Or an Irish Catholic in 1840."

The ferry sounds a final warning and pushes off toward the Statue of Liberty. Just like they did 100 years ago, people gather their belongings and get ready for the journey.

"You have to give folks a history lesson from time to time," O'Donnell shrugs. "I tell them that we all looked strange when we first got off the boat."

Central Park in the center of Manhattan

What More Did You Learn?
Discuss the following questions, based on the previous article, with a partner. Be prepared to explain your answers to the class.

1. What kind of blame have immigrants received from Americans over the years?
2. What does Ellis Island symbolize?
3. What was it like to someone who came through Ellis Island as an immigrant?
4. What is Nancy Lieggi's view of immigration?
5. What is Gary Bresson's view of immigration today?
6. How many American immigrants were African slaves?
7. How much has the Native American population declined between the years 1500 and 1900?
8. What does Jake Reinhold believe we should do with immigrants?
9. What were some attitudes toward immigration late in the nineteenth and early in the twentieth centuries? How do they compare to some attitudes today?
10. According to Evelyn Baker, what's wrong with immigration in California today?
11. Why were the Irish considered to be an unassimilable group in the nineteenth century?
12. Why were some businessmen supportive of immigration in the nineteenth century?
13. What does Ed O'Donnell offer as a possible solution to improving immigration problems today?

Analyze It
Discuss the following questions with a group or a partner.

1. Why do you think millions of people have immigrated to the United States?
2. Americans have always found reasons to oppose immigration. How might you be able to overcome some of the fears discussed in this article? With your group or partner, devise a list of criteria that must be adhered to by all immigrants.
3. Ellis Island lies in New York Harbor and, as a result, many immigrants settled and spent their lives in this city. Why do you think they chose New York over some of the other areas in the United States?

Tell Us More about It
Prepare an oral or a written report on one of the following topics. Use the outline below to organize your presentation and take notes while researching.

Giovani da Verrazano	Harlem
Henry Hudson	poverty in New York
New Amsterdam	Metropolitan Museum of Art
slavery in America	Carnegie Hall
Wall Street	Statue of Liberty
Ellis Island	Dutch West India Company

Topic:

Major points to discuss about this topic:

1.

2.

3.

4.

Details to discuss about each major point:
Major Point 1

Major Point 2

Major Point 3

Major Point 4

Tapescripts

Phoenix, Arizona

According to an ancient Egyptian legend, every five hundred years a bird called the phoenix rises from its ashes to live again. From the ancient ruins of the Hohokam Native American settlement rose the city of Phoenix, the present capital of the state of Arizona.

Until about A.D. 1450, the Hohokam tribe of Native Americans inhabited the area in the southwestern United States that is now Phoenix. They lived in a farming society that had an advanced system of irrigation, and they also introduced cotton and weaving to the southwest. Although the mystery of their disappearance has never been solved, tourists can still find ruins, canals, and artifacts of their ancient culture.

Early Spanish explorers entered the area by the 1500s. Although they left cattle and horses there, the Spanish quickly moved on to other areas because they did not find much gold. It wasn't until the mid-1850s that settlers began arriving from the eastern United States to the Phoenix area, which is on the banks of the Salt River. Because an irrigation system had been built by the Hohokams in the desert region, several ranches were established, and the settlement became a permanent one. It wasn't until after the Civil War, however, that Phoenix began to grow with any significance.

About that time, gold was rumored to be in areas around the settlement of Phoenix. Although some people seeking fortunes made the adventurous trip west, many were discouraged by hazards of the long journey. But, in 1865, the United States Army arrived to build Camp McDowell. In 1867, Jack Swilling, a former soldier, initiated farming in the Phoenix area. Soon after, the popularity of ranching, farming of very large pieces of land, began to grow as the region became safer for its inhabitants. Swilling used the old Hohokam canals to direct water to the first of his wheat and barley crops. His success attracted thirty more farmers the following year, and soon the town of Phoenix was officially formed. In 1870, the new downtown was planned and built, with real estate lots selling for twenty to one hundred and forty dollars apiece. Because wood was scarce in the area, clay adobe-style buildings were built instead. As the settlers became more prosperous, they built more elaborate Victorian-style homes.

In 1889, Phoenix was declared the capital of Arizona. It was firmly established as the business, political, and agricultural center of the territory in the southwestern United States. Because Phoenix is a desert community, it has always needed to conserve water for its residents. The Roosevelt Dam, completed in 1911, has assured water for the continued prosperity of the city.

In the 1940s, the quiet city of Phoenix developed into a center for industry and aviation training, which significantly aided the war effort. Since then, Phoenix has attracted people from all types of businesses and industries. The invention of air conditioning made the summer heat of Phoenix, which can get as hot as one hundred and twenty degrees Fahrenheit in the months of July and August, bearable for its residents. Major manufacturing and service industries now dominate the economy of the city, but agriculture is still important. Farmers there produce citrus fruits, cotton, melons, and beets and other vegetables.

Many of the original artifacts from the Phoenix area can now be found in its museums. The Heard Museum houses a collection devoted to the civilizations of Native American tribes that have lived in the area, and the Phoenix Art Museum houses a wonderful collection of western American art.

Known as the Valley of the Sun because of its warm climate and average of three hundred days of sunshine each year, the Phoenix area attracts many retired people seeking to enjoy the relaxing and healthful atmosphere of the city. Completely surrounded by a series of impressive mountains, Phoenix is one of the most naturally attractive cities in the country and inviting because of its desert culture.

Vancouver, British Columbia

Vancouver, a shining city with glorious mountains towering on its eastern side and the glimmering waterway of Georgia Strait hugging the west, has grown from being Canada's last frontier to an ideal example of Canada's mosaic culture. From the arrival of Spanish and English explorers in the 1790s to the present, Vancouver has consistently attracted a variety of immigrants, mostly from Britain and Asia. Located on Canada's southwestern coast, metropolitan Vancouver claims approximately one million six hundred thousand people, while the city proper is home to nearly half a million residents, making Vancouver Canada's third largest city.

Native Canadians were probably in the Vancouver area as early as 500 B.C. They mostly fished, hunted, and gathered food and resources there until the first European fur traders arrived in force in the 1820s. It was the native Squamish and Musqueam who first greeted and traded with Captain George Vancouver, for whom the city was later named. Vancouver explored the area in 1792 and declared it would be the most beautiful place imaginable.

With the discovery of gold in the 1850s, the natives were almost permanently dislodged. While not all of the new European settlers found riches in Vancouver, many did remain to cash in on the abundant salmon in the area waters. Known as the settlement of Granville, the area boasted many great natural resources, but the terrain was so rugged that it did not attract a great number of additional settlers over the next twenty years. But by 1886, there were twenty-five hundred settlers, with half as many natives, and three hundred wooden houses. On April 6 of that same year, Granville was incorporated as a city and had its name changed to honor Captain Vancouver, the man who first charted the area. However, with ample kindling in its structures, the new city was ripe for the fire that consumed it in twenty minutes on June 13. But the spirit of the new Vancouverites overcame this tragedy, and the city began to rebuild within days of the fire. It was also the year that welcomed the arrival of the Canadian Pacific Railroad and led to the city's growth by leaps and bounds; just twenty-five years later, the number of people who resided in the Vancouver metropolitan area had risen to over one hundred thousand.

With a serious economic depression affecting all of North America in the 1890s, Vancouver's growth slowed dramatically, but by 1897, the city found excitement once again when the Klondike Gold Rush brought fortune seekers through the city on their way north. With this boost, Vancouver surpassed Victoria, British Columbia, by the end of the century to become Canada's leading commercial center on the West Coast.

By 1914, Vancouver's growth was steady, boosted again by increased seaport activity resulting from the opening of the Panama Canal. The canal opened Vancouver to the exporting of fish, grain, and lumber to eastern Canada, the United States, and Europe. Many immigrant workers found jobs in these industries at that time.

Slowed down only a bit by World War I, Vancouver replaced Winnipeg, Manitoba, as Canada's leading western city by the end of the 1920s. The city had grown and annexed surrounding areas to the east and south, and, with the completion of the Lion's Gate Bridge in 1938, Vancouver was linked to the north, allowing easier accessibility to the city and surrounding areas. The bridge was actually built by the Guinness Brewing Company, which owned a lot of land on the other side and wanted people to do business with the company.

Although people of Asian descent have been settling in the area since the end of the nineteenth century, the European population has always dominated the politics and social atmosphere of the city. Sadly, some hostility existed early in the city's history toward people of non-British origin. In 1887 there was an anti-Chinese rally, and then in 1914, what became known as the *Komagatu Maru* incident occurred. One hundred and fifty East Indian Sikh passengers of the *Komagatu Maru* were refused entry into Vancouver after having waited on their ship for more than three months.

Vancouver has made huge strides in welcoming immigrants since that earlier time. Today it is home to a myriad of ethnic groups, with an extremely high percentage of people of Chinese descent, particularly former residents of Hong Kong, who have been waiting to see what happens to their homeland with its return to The People's Republic of China. In fact, Vancouver now claims the third largest Chinatown in North America, after San Francisco's and New York's. With a Chinese population of over three hundred thousand in metropolitan Vancouver, the city has acquired a distinctively Chinese atmosphere in other neighborhoods as well.

Vancouver was able to celebrate its diversity during its spectacular world's fair, Expo 86. As the largest special category world's fair ever in North America, including pavilions sponsored by more than one hundred countries, corporations, states, and provinces, Expo 86 was truly a celebration of the spirit of congeniality beaming from the city and its residents.

Expo 86 allowed visitors to experience not only the wonders of its pavilions but also the treats of the city. Stanley Park, one thousand acres of relaxation, was based on the ideas of Frederick Law Olmsted, designer of New York's Central Park. It is home to the National Geographic Tree, a red cedar believed to be the largest of its kind in the world. Also fun to visit is Granville Island, with its many shops and old-fashioned fresh produce marketplace. In Gastown, the quaintest part of the city, with gas lamps lining its way, one can find the Gastown Steam Clock, the only one of its kind in the world.

Throughout the 1990s, Vancouver's economy has been boosted by the film industry, which ranks Vancouver as the third largest production center in North America after Los Angeles and New York. Employing over four thousand people, the industry brings in two hundred and fifty million dollars annually to the economy of metropolitan Vancouver.

Framed by its glorious mountains that look as if they are going to fall into the sea at any moment, Vancouver is certainly a breathtaking sight for those who first lay eyes on it. With its temperate climate, friendly people, and diverse culture, it surely earns a reputation as Canada's jewel of the west and "the world within a city."

Philadelphia, Pennsylvania

The area that is today Philadelphia was first settled by the Swedes in the 1630s, who dubbed it New Sweden. In 1681, the colony of Pennsylvania was given to William Penn by King Charles II of Great Britain as a place where the people of his Quaker religion could enjoy the freedom of religious worship, have the chance to govern themselves, and develop their own way of life. Following this inspiration, Pennsylvania soon became a haven for people of all religions—Jews, Roman Catholics, and others who wanted to escape the religious persecution in Europe. Penn named the capital Philadelphia, using the Greek word meaning "city of brotherly love." Following the laying out of the city in 1682, Philadelphia quickly became a city of commerce, exporting many agricultural products to England and the West Indies. In return, from the West Indies it received sugar, molasses, and rum. So successful was it commercially that by the middle of the eighteenth century, Philadelphia was trading even more goods than Boston.

Industry blossomed as trade increased in the growing city. Leather and shipbuilding became large industries, as did flour milling, paper production, and rum making. Benjamin Franklin, one of the most prominent of America's founding fathers, rose as a leader in scientific and intellectual affairs in Philadelphia, founding the nation's first free library and first hospital. With his strong influence, as well as that of physician Benjamin Rush, sculptor William Rush, and painter Benjamin West, Philadelphia became a cultural center that rivaled Boston. Because of its location along the eastern seaboard, its size, and its importance among the American colonies, it was chosen as the site to host the First Continental Congress when problems began with Great Britain in the mid-eighteenth century.

The founding fathers convened in Philadelphia at Independence Hall in 1776 to sign the "Declaration of Independence" from Great Britain. The wealthy nobleman from Boston, John Hancock, signed his name in very large letters, reportedly so that King George could read it without his glasses.

During the American Revolution that followed, Philadelphia was occupied by British troops in the winter of 1777–78. After the British left the city, the Continental Congress returned and voted to temporarily establish Philadelphia as the center of the nation's government until a permanent capital was found.

Following the financial hardship of the Revolutionary War, the economy of Philadelphia recovered quickly. The shipyards were building ships of exceptional quality, which made it easier for traders from the city to begin exploring the riches of Europe and China. As a result, Philadelphia exported more manufactured goods than any other city in the new nation during this time. By the end of the eighteenth century, Philadelphia had evolved into the largest city in the United States and the third largest in the English-speaking world!

Even from colonial times, there was a large population of free African Americans in Philadelphia. This allowed the city to develop into a natural center for the anti-slavery movement during the nineteenth century. Even so, this movement caused tensions to mount between the two racial groups, leading to white uprisings, between 1829 and 1860, against the abolitionists, who were fighting against the slavery of blacks.

By the 1830s, Philadelphia had lost its prominence as a center of politics, culture, commerce, and finance. Traders preferred the large, growing port of New York. Still, Philadelphia's economic activity was boosted once again when the Pennsylvania Railroad completed a line to Pittsburgh, Pennsylvania, from Philadelphia in 1854, allowing for increased regional trade. After the American Civil War, a war between the North and the South, Philadelphians and other Americans were drawn to the excitement of the Centennial Exposition in 1876, one of the first great world's fairs, whose main focus was the display of U.S. technological advances.

During the nineteenth century many immigrant groups—Irish, Italian, Polish, and others—arrived in Philadelphia. And by the beginning of the twentieth century, Philadelphia had the largest African American population of any northern city in the United States. Many white city residents left the city in favor of the suburbs during the middle of this century, leading to an African American population of nearly forty percent by the 1980s, while ninety-five percent of the suburban population was white.

The downtown section of today's Philadelphia is the oldest part of the city. It's on a peninsula surrounded by the Delaware River to the east and south and the Schuylkill River to the west. "The Cradle of the Nation", as Philadelphia is often referred to because of its important contribution in the formation of the nation, has become a popular tourist attraction due to the restoration of historic buildings in the downtown area following the country's bicentennial celebration in 1976. Independence Hall, the Liberty Bell Pavilion, and Carpenter's Hall, where the First Continental Congress met, along with other buildings used during the American Revolution and by the early federal government can be visited by tourists in this area.

A city filled with the historical values of the early nation, Philadelphia is today a vibrant cultural center.

Honolulu, Hawaii

Aloha, and welcome to Honolulu! Located on the southeastern coast of the Hawaiian island of Oahu in the Pacific Ocean, Honolulu is the largest city and capital of the Hawaiian Islands, the fiftieth state of the United States. The city lies along ten miles of coastline and reaches four miles inland to the foothills of the Koolau Mountain Range. Called the Crossroads of the Pacific, Honolulu is the chief port for the islands in the Pacific Ocean, being twenty-four hundred miles from San Francisco, California, and thirty-eight hundred miles from Tokyo, Japan. Home to about eighty percent of the population of Hawaii, Honolulu is a destination for tourists from all over the world who want to enjoy the warmth of the tropical sun, the luxury of the sandy beaches, and Hawaii's welcoming Polynesian culture.

Honolulu was first settled by Polynesians centuries ago, when it was given its present name, which means "sheltered bay." It may have been as early as A.D. 1100 that the original settlers arrived on the island. It wasn't until 1794, when Captain William Brown, an English seaman, sailed into what is now Honolulu Harbor to seek food and shelter, that Europeans made any significant influence on the islands. Honolulu was then a small Polynesian village, but it soon became an important port when other European ships started to stop there on their voyages across the Pacific.

During the 1800s, Honolulu became important as a commercial whaling base in the Pacific Ocean under the rule of King Kamehameha I, the first ruler of Hawaii, who lived in Honolulu from 1803 to 1811. In the 1820s, Protestant missionaries from New England arrived in Honolulu with the purpose of converting the Hawaiian people to Christianity. They built schools and churches that resembled the architecture of New England. The European influence continued to grow so much that in 1843 the port of Honolulu was occupied by the British, and then by the French in 1849. It was then returned to King Kamehameha III, who in 1850 declared Honolulu his capital. Under his rule, industry grew, and by the end of the nineteenth century, farmers had begun to have success growing pineapples and sugar-cane on the islands. This attracted many laborers from Japan, China, and other countries, resulting in a population for Honolulu of nearly thirty thousand people by 1836, including natives, Europeans, and Asians.

The United States Navy began establishing a military presence near Honolulu in the early 1900s, which increased Honolulu's population to over one hundred and thirty thousand by 1930. People from Japan, China, and other Asian countries had long been kept out of politics and business in Honolulu. However, after World War II, many Americans of Asian descent became strong leaders of Honolulu's politics and businesses.

With a lot of growth in the first half of the twentieth century, Hawaii took a giant step into its future in 1959, when it became the fiftieth state of the United States, with Honolulu as its capital. The popularity of air travel after this time allowed Honolulu to become one of the world's top tourist destinations. Many high-rise apartment buildings and luxury hotels were built along the ocean to accommodate tourists. By 1992, nearly six and a half million tourists were visiting Honolulu each year.

Today, seventy percent of the people of Honolulu are of Japanese, Chinese, or Filipino ancestry, and nearly thirty percent are white. Only about eight percent of the people are Hawaiian or part Hawaiian. American military personnel and their families make up about fifteen percent of Honolulu's population. Because of this diverse population, Honolulu is today a center for the study of Pacific culture. The Bernice P. Bishop Museum has a large collection of Polynesian art and artifacts, helping to preserve the island's distinctive past.

The city also has many historical and naturally beautiful sights for tourists to visit. Pearl Harbor, the first naval base on the island of Oahu, is located on the western shore of the city. The bombing of

Pearl Harbor on December 7, 1941 made the islands of Hawaii better known to the rest of the United States and made Pearl Harbor a center for military activity during World War II, the Korean War, and the Vietnam War. Diamond Head, an extinct, or nonactive, volcano, is at the eastern end of the city, creating a serene backdrop for the Honolulu skyline. The Koolau Mountains rise north of the downtown area, providing a dramatic backdrop for the famous beaches and the resort area of Waikiki. The Iolani Palace, the former capitol and royal palace of the Hawaiian monarchs, stands across the street from the new Hawaiian state capitol building.

The economy of Honolulu, and of the rest of the Hawaiian Islands, depends largely on the income spent by the U.S. military personnel, followed closely by the fast-growing tourist industry. Because Honolulu's average temperature is 72 degrees Fahrenheit in February, the coldest month, and 78 degrees Fahrenheit in August and September, the warmest months, millions of tourists come from all over the world to enjoy the luxury of the area. Most tourists stay in the Waikiki Beach area, but developers are now building resorts in other parts of the city to lessen the overcrowding in Waikiki. Visiting Honolulu, Hawaii, is like visiting paradise on Earth. The United States is lucky to call the city one of its gems.

Side Trip: Hawaii Volcanoes National Park

Aloha again, and welcome to the Big Island of Hawaii, home to Hawaii Volcanoes National Park and the world's largest active volcano. It is also home, believe it or not, to the largest mountain on Earth! The biggest island in the Hawaiian Island chain, Hawaii, referred to affectionately as the "Big Island," is home to five volcanoes, three of which have been active over the last two centuries. Here you can see the world in creation, lava flowing almost continuously out of the craters of Kilauea.

The most recent eruption from Kilauea started in January 1983 and continues today. It has been one of the most studied volcanoes in the world because of its glacierlike eruptions. Because the volcano oozes lava slowly from cracks on its side, rather than emitting gas or causing explosions like other volcanoes, it is safe for most visitors and scientists to observe from nearby. Built in 1912, the Hawaiian Volcano Observatory , which sits on top of Kilauea, has been keeping an eye on all the activity from the volcano's center. One of the most interesting recent developments has been the creation of a lava lake in July 1986. It measures one acre in size and is one hundred and eighty feet deep, filled with red hot lava. At the end of April 1987, the lava started flowing more aggressively out of the lake and destroyed homes and other structures, causing more than twenty-five million dollars in damage.

Mauna Loa, meaning "Long Mountain," occupies the entire southern half of the Big Island and is Kilauea's neighbor. Containing more than 10,000 cubic miles of lava, the volcano claims to be the most massive mountain on Earth. Measured from its base eighteen thousand feet below sea level to its peak, the volcano would even top Mount Everest! Like Kilauea, it has also been erupting over the last couple of centuries, but rarely at the same time as Kilauea. The last significant eruption was in April 1984. It seems Kilauea and Mauna Loa like to take turns spewing their fury!

According to Hawaiian legend, the goddess Madame Pele makes her home at Halemaumau Crater at the south end of Kilauea. Whenever Pele is upset by life's pressure, she blows her top and lets lava flow out of the sides of her volcano home. Natives have tried to appease her over the years by leaving offerings of pigs, berries, and even her personal favorite, gin! She considers the lava rocks found around the Big Island her children and will cast bad luck on anyone who takes them home. So, be careful next time you visit the home of Madame Pele on the Big Island and be good to her. Aloha for now!

Los Angeles, California

Known as the land of the sun, Los Angeles, California, was founded by the Spanish in 1781 near the Native American village of Yang-na. Since then it has been known as a promised land, health haven, movie capital, and a world financial center. The second largest city in the United States, Los Angeles is surrounded by five mountain ranges and the Pacific Ocean, with many sandy beaches and beautiful hills within its borders.

At the time of its founding, Los Angeles was only a small settlement of forty-four people, but it grew under Mexican rule as the temporary capital of California. Named El Pueblo de la Reina de Los Angeles (the Town of the Queen of the Angels) by the Spanish governor of California, Felipe de Neva, it was later shortened by the inhabitants to simply Los Angeles, meaning "the angels." The first settlers were a mixture of Spaniards, Native Americans, people of mixed blood, and African Americans, many of whom were women and children. They farmed the land and prospered over the next fifty years.

The Indians who originally populated the area of Los Angeles were converted by the Spaniards to Catholicism and forced to become slaves. They helped the Spaniards build religious missions along the coast of California. With the Indian slaves dying in large numbers and the Spanish government involved in too many other overseas projects, Mexico declared its independence from Spain in 1821 and claimed California as its own. The city, however, was later captured by Americans during the Mexican War in 1846. Since then it has been governed by the United States, but a large number of its inhabitants are still of Mexican descent.

During the late 1840s, many easterners traveled to California in search of gold. The California Gold Rush started in northern California, near San Francisco and Sacramento, but some of the miners moved down to Los Angeles in search of their fortune. The settlement was then a small, rough cow town that averaged one murder each day. But the influx of people allowed it to grow and develop into a more lawful town. By the time the railroad arrived in Los Angeles in 1869, it was still a small city in comparison to those in northern California.

During the 1870s, magazines and newspapers reported on Los Angeles's history and beauty, which attracted a large number of new settlers and visitors. When the railroad finally reached the resort coastal area of Santa Monica, next to Los Angeles, the city began to develop as a major shipping port. With the discovery of oil in the region in the early twentieth century, many of the inhabitants of Los Angeles turned to the newly invented automobile for quick transportation. Ever since, the residents of the Los Angeles community have depended heavily on their cars to get around. Because Los Angeles lacks a good mass transportation system, its main highways are often filled with traffic going nowhere.

More than anything else, the city has long been known as the movie capital of the world. The motion picture industry started in Los Angeles in about 1910, attracted by the variety in the physical characteristics of the landscape and the sunny, mild weather. With the advances of technology, which have made business easier, most of the television and movie industry remains in and around the city of Los Angeles. Many of the most popular tourist attractions include homes of movie stars in the fashionable city of Beverly Hills, which borders Los Angeles, and the movie studios throughout the area.

Although Los Angeles remains a home for many industries and all types of people, earthquakes are still a major threat to the region. Many small earthquakes rattle the area each year, with the last large quake hitting in 1994. The strongest earthquake to hit Los Angeles occurred in the 1850s when almost every building in the young city was destroyed. Residents of Los Angeles and the surrounding southern California region are still awaiting the "big one," the major earthquake that some experts speculate might make California disappear into the ocean or separate from the U.S. mainland.

Still, Los Angeles is unique in that it is a city that is still growing. It attracts all kinds of people with all kinds of dreams. The largest ethnic group is Hispanics, most of whom are of Mexican descent. Asians make up the next largest group, and they have developed some of their own sections of the city, such as Chinatown and Little Tokyo.

With so many people and industries in an area with so much sunshine, the air quality of the Los Angeles region has suffered. Even with the unhealthy layer of smog over the city, millions of people still happily live in, work in, and visit the area each year. To some people, Los Angeles is Tinseltown, to others it's Smogsville, the Rome of the West, or the City of Angels. No matter how it is known, it definitely offers something for everyone.

Miami, Florida

Miami, Florida, the southernmost major city in the United States, is located on the southeastern coast of Florida along the Atlantic Ocean. While the city itself has a population of only three hundred and seventy thousand people, the metropolitan area of Miami has a population of almost two million. Because of the warm climate, its location on the ocean, and the number of resorts available, Miami has become one of the greatest tourist destinations in the world, attracting millions of people each year.

The name of the city probably comes from the Indian word meaning "Big Water." This refers to the immense Lake Okeechobee, northwest of the city. Maps from the sixteenth century show an Indian village inhabited by the Calusa and Tequesta Native American tribes in what is now downtown Miami.

The Spanish explorer Ponce de Leon first set foot in Miami in 1513. Fort Dallas, which is located near the mouth of the Miami River, was built in 1836 during battles with the Seminole Indians. In 1896, the East Coast Railroad was extended to Miami as a result of urging by the pioneer settlers in the region. At that time, there were not many more than a few dwellings near the abandoned Fort Dallas, but soon the new railroad encouraged progress in the area, attracting curious people from the northern United States. Henry Flagler, who had built the railroad, also opened the first luxury hotel, the Royal Palm Hotel. Still little more than a fishing village, the city of Miami was incorporated that same year.

It wasn't until the 1920s, however, that real estate developers began to see the potential Miami had to offer as a place to live. Men called "Binder Boys" stood on the street corners selling inexpensive real estate. Thousands of people turned into millionaires overnight from real estate purchases. More started heading to Miami to build homes and businesses in this huge land boom, but in 1926, the destruction caused by a severe hurricane frightened people from settling in the Miami area. Nearly four hundred people were killed and thousands of buildings destroyed. Despite all this, the region did continue to grow in the following years as swampland was drained and parks were created. After the Great Depression, in the mid-1930s, there was an incredible growth in the building of hotels along the southern end of Miami Beach. These hotels were built in the art deco style of architecture, painted in bright pastel colors and designed with geometric lines. As a result, thousands of tourists began visiting the area each year.

The diverse groups that reside in Miami, including white Americans, Caribbean islanders, and Latin Americans, were attracted there for various reasons. During the 1930s and 1940s, Miami was a haven for the rich and elite. Many movie stars visited the beaches and enjoyed the area. Then, in the mid-1940s, Miami began to attract many older settlers who wanted to escape the cold winters in the northern United States.

Because Miami has had the image of being a land of promise, many Cuban refugees have settled there since 1960. The city's large population is now made up of nearly a quarter of a million people of Cuban heritage. This group has grown from an influx of three hundred thousand refugees who arrived in the area shortly after Fidel Castro took power in Cuba in 1959. Then, more came in 1980 as a result of Castro's release of Cubans wanting to leave their homeland. Many of these immigrants settled in what has become known as the "Little Havana" section of Miami. Today Central and South Americans also enjoy the climate and culture in the Miami area. In fact, Spanish is spoken as much as English in the city today. This new Latin flavor has changed every aspect of Miami—its food, music, fashion, architecture, and media. Not surprisingly, the Latin Americans tend to dominate the politics of the area as well.

Miami is not only diverse in ethnic makeup, it is also home to many art museums. Villa Vizcaya is an Italian Renaissance–style palazzo built by industrialist James Deering and houses the Dade County Art Museum. Just outside of Miami lies the Everglades National Park. It offers people the opportunity to observe natural beauty and unspoiled wilderness. Off the east coast of the city is a string of islands known as Miami Beach, home to many of the luxury resorts in the area and some of the most beautiful beaches in the United States.

More than ten million tourists visit the Miami area each year. They generate over sixty percent of Miami's economic activity. To best serve these tourists, ten percent of Miami's population is involved in restaurant and hotel businesses around the city. The city is fast becoming the tropical capital of the United States. It's the perfect place to enjoy the sun, the luxurious warmth of the Atlantic Ocean, and an international atmosphere.

Las Vegas, Nevada

With a population of two hundred fifty-eight thousand, Las Vegas, Nevada, is a city known worldwide for its nightclub entertainment and gambling casinos. Located in southeastern Nevada, about two hundred miles east of Los Angeles, California, Las Vegas is a year-round desert resort. The city entertains millions of guests each year, is a major convention center in the United States, and is the center for commercial and mining activity in the southwestern region of the country.

Because of the dominance of the gambling industry in Las Vegas, it is hard to believe there is much history associated with it. But history does exist here, and once it's found, the history explains a lot about this unique town. Discovered by Europeans in 1829, Las Vegas was visited by the Pueblo Native American tribe as early as 300 B.C. In 1829, a group of traders, led by a New Mexican named Antonio Armijo, decided to shorten its trip along the Old Spanish Trail from Santa Fe, New Mexico, to Los Angeles, California, by traveling north of the Colorado River. But they almost ran out of water, so Armijo sent a young Mexican scout named Raphael Rivera to search for an oasis, which is a spot in the desert where there is water and vegetation. Rivera returned thirteen days later with news that he had found a spot with plenty of water and huge green meadows. The Spanish called this place, las vegas, which meant "the meadows." The traders took advantage of the fresh water and well-deserved rest in the meadows, then set out for Los Angeles, which they reached less than three weeks later.

Soon after Armijo's expedition, other Western explorers arrived in the region. In 1855, a group of Mormon missionaries who had been sent by their leader, Brigham Young, as guides for those seeking gold in California, came to Las Vegas. Young's Mormon Church claimed much of the land west of the Colorado River, calling the area Deseret. Because of the plentiful water there, the group thought Las Vegas was a good place to stop on their way from Salt Lake City, Utah, to southern California, because it was located perfectly between the two cities. When they arrived there one month after leaving Salt Lake City, the Mormon missionaries immediately started to build a large adobe fort to protect and house themselves.

Farming almost became an important part of Las Vegas's history as the Mormons began to farm the area near the water springs. However, it was the discovery of lead on Mount Potosi, thirty-five miles southwest of the city, that distracted the Mormons from their farming work. Less than two years after Brigham Young had sent his missionaries to Las Vegas, he closed the mission and moved his followers to Mount Potosi. Although they didn't get rich from the lead, the Mormons gained valuable experience in mining, which they put to use more successfully in southern Utah.

The San Pedro, Los Angeles, and Salt Lake Railroad, which went through Las Vegas, had been started in 1902 by Senator William Clark. On April 15, 1905, the first train carried vacationers to Las Vegas. The railroad helped encourage new interest in mining the land south of town. More settlers arrived hoping to get rich, which helped the city reach a population of fifteen hundred people by 1911, when it was incorporated as a city.

The original railroad station, once located at the end of Fremont Street, was the center for social and economic life until the late 1930s. It was torn down in 1940 to make room for the Union Plaza Hotel. Still standing in that area today is the Victory Hotel, built in 1910, overshadowed by the modern Golden Nugget Hotel and Casino on North Main Street.

The gambling casinos are the heart of Las Vegas. Gambling, which was legal in most western states during the nineteenth century, was outlawed in Nevada in 1915. However, a decline in the success of mining during the Great Depression around 1930 led local political leaders to consider making gambling legal again. So, in 1931, open gambling and less stringent divorce laws were passed to raise money for the state. Since then, Las Vegas has grown incredibly because of the casino industry. It grew so much that the Hoover Dam was built in the mid-1930s to save water for the growing Las Vegas area. Las Vegas also began to attract couples from southern California, and other nearby regions, who were seeking quick marriages or divorces. Today, the city even has some drive-up wedding chapels for those couples in more of a hurry!

Benjamin "Bugsy" Siegel, the gangster and casino owner, is the one person most associated with the history of Las Vegas and the gambling industry. Siegel arrived in Las Vegas from the eastern United States in the late 1930s. He saw the city as a potential gold mine for gambling. In 1942, having already started some small gambling businesses in Las Vegas, Siegel quickly eliminated his competition. With his profits and economic backing from other sources, Siegel started construction of his own luxury casino, the incredible Flamingo Hotel, which was finished in 1946. Situated on a piece of land next to the Los Angeles Highway, the Flamingo Hotel forever changed the focus of life in Las Vegas to gambling and glitz. Although Siegel was shot in his Beverly Hills, California, home in 1947, his legacy lives on in fancy casinos like Caesars Palace and the Sands.

Today the chief tourist attraction in Las Vegas is gambling, but developers have been adding more theme park-type attractions in recent years in hopes of luring families with children. The major casinos and attractions are at the downtown Casino Center and on the Strip, which is a stretch of highway leading into the city. The casinos, many of which are located in luxury hotels, operate twenty-four hours a day. At night, the bright, multicolored neon signs light up the desert sky, giving Las Vegas its unique multicolored skyline.

Side Trip: The Grand Canyon

Not very far away from Las Vegas, Nevada, to the southeast, in the state of Arizona, is the spectacular natural rock formation of the five million year–old Grand Canyon, formed by erosion from the Colorado River that runs through it. At 277 miles long and nearly a mile deep, it is not the deepest canyon in the world, but the Grand Canyon is one of the most famous because of its spectacular colorful vistas, its valuable record of American geological history, with layers of ancient rock and wonderful examples of erosion. It's especially noted for its spectacular colors, which, depending on the time of day and brightness of the sun, range from a deep red to green and pink and brown and gray in its deepest parts.

Although Native Americans had wandered through the canyon regularly for thousands of years, Spanish explorer Garcia Lopez de Cardenas was the first European to view the canyon in 1540. Then, in 1869, John Wesley Powell took a group through the canyon and told one of the most remembered tales of travel of early western America. By the 1870s, many others followed, and the Grand Canyon had become a well-explored area. In 1919, the Grand Canyon became a United States National Park in order to receive the best protection the nation can offer, to open the park for visitors to enjoy and learn from, and to preserve it in its natural state for future generations.

Although most of the visible rocks are fairly young in geological terms, some of the oldest formations date back nearly four billion years and can tell us a great deal about the formation of our planet. Most visitors come to the canyon via the south rim and may hike down or ride mules to the Colorado River. Others may venture through the canyon on a river raft trip or just enjoy the spectacular view from the rim. In recent years, the colors of the canyon have actually been enhanced by air pollution caused by particles emitted from nearby factories. They may view ruins in the cliffs that indicate prehistoric occupation by different tribes. Even today, several Native Americans live on nearby reservations.

Remember, though, if you plan a trip to the Grand Canyon, the weather can vary quite a bit from season to season. In summer, the temperatures at the rim can be quite comfortable, but it might be well over 100 degrees Fahrenheit at the bottom. In winter, snowfall may obscure the view and make the rim a pretty cold place to wander about. Most of all, if you plan to hike down one of the many canyon trails, remember to bring plenty of water and food and you'll be guaranteed to have one of the most amazing experiences of your life.

Montréal, Québec

French explorer Jacques Cartier sailed down the St. Lawrence River in 1535 and came upon an island in what is today southern Québec, Canada, just north of New York State. The native inhabitants of the island, the Hurons, called their home Hochelaga, but Cartier dubbed it Mont Réal after the great hill that rose up in the center of the island. Today a large metropolis, Montréal started as a small fur trading post and France's claim in the New World.

It wasn't until seventy years after Cartier first arrived here that another explorer happened upon the lonely island. Samuel de Champlain stayed for a while and worked the earth of the island but didn't stay long enough for a permanent settlement to be established, which happened in 1642 with the arrival of French missionaries under the direction of Paul de Chomedey, Sieur de Maisonneuve. Maisonneuve and his group called their village Ville-Marie and built a sturdy fortress of logs, and later stone, to protect themselves from the frequent attacks by the native peoples of the area.

Most of the missionaries were men, so the colony didn't grow very much until town leaders arranged for women to be brought from France to marry the male inhabitants of Montréal. These women, called the daughters of the king, were brought by the boatload to the province. In fact, the leaders wanted the city to grow so much that they actually fined bachelors who did not take a wife within two hours after the women disembarked from their ships. This wasn't a joke, as a man's fur trading license could have been taken away if he didn't choose a bride, leading to a lack of livelihood!

Very much a proud French town in its early years, Montréal was taken over by the British in 1760 after the French and Indian War, which pitted the French, and the natives who fought with them, against the American colonists and the British. However, the strong vitality of the French culture has prevailed ever since, due in large part to the Québec Act of 1774, which allowed both English and

French settlers to keep their own languages, religions, and cultures. When hostilities broke out in the American colonies to the south in the 1770s, British sympathizers traveled northward to Montréal to seek refuge in a politically friendly area.

Montréal grew rapidly from this time, and by the nineteenth century it was expanding quickly over the whole island and across the river. In 1809, steamship service was established along the St. Lawrence River, and during the 1830s and 1840s train connections to New York, Boston, and Toronto were established, both bringing increased business activity to the city. By 1892, Montréalers were able to get around more easily on an electric tramway built in the heart of downtown.

Around this same time, more immigrants from various parts of the world began arriving in Montréal. Ethnic neighborhoods were established, and the various groups lived happily together. Even today, most Montréalers speak at least two languages.

Montréal has continued to grow during the twentieth century and has made every effort to guard its French heritage. In 1967, the city exhibited its pride at Expo '67 and invited the rest of the world to Montréal with the theme of "Man and His World." Then again, in 1976, the world came to Montréal when the summer Olympic Games were held. Montréal Olympic Park is still preserved today as a place for Montréalers and tourists alike and as a reminder of the international quality the Games brought to this unique city.

A few years after this, French Montréalers joined the rest of Québec in reminding their country of their uniqueness. Even though Montréal is the second largest French city in the world after Paris, the French felt as if their culture and language were disappearing under a heavy blanket of English Canadian control. Led by the dominant Parti Québecois, the Province of Québec has twice tried unsuccessfully to separate from Canada and become a country of its own. Although the group has lost its dream of an independent French culture in North America for the time being, because of the close results of the referendums, it has reminded the rest of Canada that the French language and culture are something special and should be guarded before they are lost forever. All street signs in Montréal are in French, and radio stations are required to play a certain percentage of French music for their listeners.

Hidden under a heavy blanket of snow during its long winters, Montréal has always brought a unique quality to its country of Canada. Ice hockey is second nature to most young Quebecers, along with rich food to help get them through the bone-chilling winters. But when spring arrives, Montréalers are out in force and tourists flock to the island. The Montréal Jazz Festival is held each year and is known for its superb quality of musicians. Other charming areas to visit are Old Montréal, the home of the early settlers, and St. Catherine Street, where great shopping can be done.

Ever strong in spirit and culture, Montréal offers a visitor a wealth of activities and a variety of climates to enjoy. Whether you want to ski or swim, Montréal has it all!

Washington, D.C.

Washington, D.C., the capital city of the United States, is located in the District of Columbia, surrounded by the Potomac River, Maryland, and Virginia. It is the eighth most populated city in the United States. As of 1990, more than six hundred thousand people were living in this capital city. Inhabited by U.S. politicians and hundreds of foreign diplomats, Washington is well known as a center of international political activity.

In 1608, Captain John Smith, an English investor, explored the Potomac River and the Native American villages along its banks. In 1631, Henry Fleete described the area as a major trading center for the Nacostin Indians. In 1639, Jesuit priests from Maryland established religious missions along the Potomac River, near what is today the city of Washington. By 1700, the land was given to Scottish settlers by Lord Baltimore of Great Britain.

After the American Revolution, in the 1780s and 1790s, northern and southern political leaders argued over the site for the new capital of the young country. New York City was selected temporarily, then Philadelphia. Problems arose because southerners wanted the nation's capital in the south, while northerners wanted it in the north. The northern states finally agreed to the southern location of the capital if the southern states paid the debt of the American Revolution.

The first president, George Washington, personally selected the site of the nation's permanent capital in 1791. It included land given up by the states of Maryland and Virginia. Washington selected Pierre L'Enfant, a Frenchman, to plan the city and three commissioners to be in charge of the construction. The commissioners named the city Washington, after the first president. Construction of the White House, the residence of the president and his family and the oldest public building in the city, was begun in 1792. The next year, the president laid the cornerstone for the Capitol building, and construction of the rest of the city began. Interestingly, L'Enfant indicated in his plans for the city that no building could be taller than the Capitol building, which stands on top of a hill. Even today, there are no significantly tall buildings in Washington, D.C., making it a very elegant metropolitan center.

The national government was officially transferred to Washington, D.C., in 1800. The second president, John Adams, and his wife, Abigail, were the first occupants of the White House. Because the city was still largely uninhabited and very remote, it was nicknamed "Wilderness City." In 1814, not long after its completion, the British captured Washington, D.C., and burned many of the buildings. As a result, President James Madison and his wife, Dolly, were forced to leave the city. Washington was soon reconstructed, however, giving Americans a new and stronger appreciation for their nation's capital.

During the Civil War (1861–65) when the southern part of the United States, the Confederacy, fought against the North over the issue of slavery and economics, Washington served as the major base of operations for the Union Army of the North. The city's buildings were used as headquarters and hospitals for the wounded soldiers and civilians. The war drove many freed slaves and whites into the city, doubling its population. After the war, African Americans were briefly given the right to vote, but because officials were worried about racial problems, the Congress of the United States soon took away this right. A former slave, Frederick Douglass, became the spiritual leader for the city's first civil rights movement soon after the war.

There was a steady arrival of African Americans during the beginning of the twentieth century. With little housing available to them, the African Americans crowded into the city's alleys. By 1897, the alley dwellers numbered more than seventeen thousand, causing Congress to pass the Alley Dwelling Act in 1914, which forced relocation of all who lived in the alleys. But relocation was delayed as funding for the low-income housing was difficult to secure.

More improvements were made during the Great Depression of the 1930s and during World War II, when federal jobs were created that attracted foreign immigrants to the capital city. During World War II, the city's population briefly exceeded one million.

Because it's the political center of the United States, Washington, D.C., was the site of many demonstrations over the years. In 1963, Martin Luther King, Jr., famous for his nonviolent protests for the civil rights movement, spoke passionately to an audience of more than two hundred thousand people, in his famous, "I have a dream" speech, appealing to his listeners' love of the American dream. Five years later, following his assassination, black frustrations led to violent riots. In the late 1960s and the early 1970s, Washington was the center of activity for the anti–Vietnam War movement, and ever since, it has been a center for protests and demonstrations of all kinds. In the 1980s, there was a new growth in the downtown area of the city, with the construction of a new subway and a wave of immigrants from Latin America.

Washington's present population is the most educated in the United States, with twice as many college educated adults as the national average. The city has so many museums and art galleries that it is almost impossible to see everything they contain. The nation's largest museum, the Smithsonian Institution, is actually a group of museums that includes the Air and Space Museum and the National Zoo.

The city itself is probably the greatest work of art to be observed. Examples of almost every style and period of architecture exist in Washington. Some interesting structures to view are the old Executive Office Building, the White House, and the beautiful monuments to Presidents Thomas Jefferson, Abraham Lincoln, George Washington, and Franklin Delano Roosevelt.

As the seat of the United States government, Washington plays a unique role in both national and international life. Not only is Washington the only major city in the United States to be planned, but it is also one of the most beautiful cities along the eastern seaboard. A visitor to the city shouldn't miss the chance to walk around and enjoy the long tree-lined streets, the beautiful Japanese cherry blossoms of the early spring, and above all, the sense of history displayed at every turn.

Side Trip: Colonial Williamsburg, Virginia

Located between the York and James Rivers in the state of Virginia and not too far south of Washington, D.C., the settlement of Middle Plantation was begun in 1633 to protect the peninsula from Native American attacks. Later, in 1698, this settlement served as the temporary capital of Virginia while Jamestown, the first British settlement in America, was being rebuilt after a disastrous fire. In 1699, the town was made the permanent capital and was renamed Williamsburg after King William III of England.

The town quickly became Virginia's cultural center and was the site of much pre–Revolutionary War activity by the American colonists. The oldest American college, the College of William and Mary, which dates back to 1695, is located here. However, when the capital of Virginia was moved to Richmond in 1880 because of its more central location, Williamsburg became primarily a college town. And when the college closed for eight years in 1881, Williamsburg became a forgotten town. After the college reopened in 1889 and a munitions factory was built in 1917, the city came to life once again.

In 1926, John D. Rockefeller, one of America's oil tycoons and richest men, donated money so that the original settlement of Williamsburg could be restored to its eighteenth-century splendor and so that America could look toward its future by learning from its past. Today visitors can travel back in time and experience how the earliest Americans lived as they walk through a living, working community with inhabitants going about their business as they would have in the eighteenth century. The people who bring this community to life not only wear the costumes of the time period but also embody the personalities of eighteenth-century politicians, housewives, slaves, soldiers, and patriots. Their stories will take you back in time and allow you to see how similar your lives might be to theirs, as well as how incredibly different. Their insights will allow you to understand how America has developed its system of values. They will invite you to learn their trades, eat their food, and walk through their eighteenth-century gardens. All in all, the experience of Colonial Williamsburg in Virginia, will remind you of America's past and how it became the nation it is today.

Chicago, Illinois

Chicago, located in the northwestern section of the state of Illinois, is the third most populated city in the United States. Situated on the shores of Lake Michigan on a relatively flat area of land, Chicago is today an international center for manufacturing, trade, and finance. Known widely for its notorious gangster history, blues music, deep dish pizza, and beautiful architecture, the city is also breathtaking to enjoy for shoppers and historians alike.

Because of its central location in the midwestern section of the country, Chicago has always been considered a gateway to the western United States. Because Chicago was a common Native American resting stop, most historians agree that the city got its name from the Native American word meaning "strong" or "powerful." Others reportedly argue, however, that the name can be traced to a Native American word meaning "stinking wild onions," a reference to the vegetable that grew in abundance nearby.

In 1673, French explorers Louis Jolliet and Jacques Marquette were the first Europeans to visit the area, but they did not establish a permanent settlement at that time. While many fur trappers and traders traveled through the area, it was finally Jean Baptiste Point du Sable, a French-African fur trapper, who established the first permanent settlement in what is today downtown Chicago.

At the turn of the eighteenth century, Captain John Whistler of the United States Army arrived in the area with his soldiers to build Fort Dearborn on the shores of Lake Michigan. However, at the start of the War of 1812 (fought against the British), Whistler's fort was destroyed, and most of the people inside the fort were killed by Native Americans fighting for the British, who had come south from Canada to fight. Realizing the vital importance of keeping a fort in the strategic Chicago area, the U.S. government rebuilt Fort Dearborn in 1816. With the comfort of a fort in the area, more and more new settlers began arriving. Still, the city grew very slowly until 1830, when the community was given $25,000 by the U.S. Congress to build a harbor for itself in Lake Michigan. Shortly after that, Chicago, which had only forty-three houses and two hundred inhabitants, was incorporated as a village and, by 1837, became a city.

From then on, Chicago grew at a rapid pace as a city whose economy was based primarily on trade. Most buildings were wooden and were constructed too quickly, and the streets were always filled with mud. Still, the potential of Chicago to be a great city was finally realized in 1847 when a large convention brought many businessmen to the area, some of whom decided to invest in the city's future greatness. Chicago's tradition as a convention city was strengthened in 1860 when Abraham Lincoln was nominated to be a candidate for the presidency of the United States at the Republican National Convention.

Surprisingly, during the 1860s, the Civil War, the war that divided the Southern and Northern states, brought economic prosperity to the city. Chicago factories became specialists in manufacturing and food processing for the North's cause. During and after the Civil War, the expansion of the railroads helped Chicago grow in terms of its population and economy. The Galena and Union Railway had been established in 1848, and so by 1853, Chicago had become a primary rest stop on the way to the western United States. By the end of the Civil War in 1865, the population of Chicago had risen to three hundred thousand, and the city was flourishing with activity.

Rapid growth had a downside, however. In 1871, most of the buildings in downtown Chicago were destroyed by a great fire that burned out of control from October 8 through October 10. Although no one can say for sure what started the massive fire, one famous tale blames the conflagration on Mrs. O'Leary's cow, who knocked over a lantern left by its side. Although Mrs. O'Leary's house still stood after the fire, most of the other structures downtown and on the north side of the city burned to the ground. One of the few structures left standing was the three-year-old Gothic-style water tower on the north side of the city, which has become a favorite landmark for residents and visitors alike.

While some people thought that the Great Fire would destroy Chicago's chances to be an important American city, the city was actually strengthened by the fire. Within the first week after the fire, over six thousand temporary buildings had been built. The fire actually gave the people of Chicago a chance to plan their city from scratch, with higher standards and a better design of streets than it had had previously.

Because Chicago grew as a center for manufacturing, especially after the fire, many labor disputes resulted in the 1880s and early 1890s. What has become known as the Haymarket Riots occurred in May 1886 when a bomb was thrown into a labor meeting where the introduction of an eight-hour work day was being discussed. Over one hundred fifty policemen had been called to quiet a reported riot there, but it turned deadly when seven policemen lost their lives. Later in the 1890s, hard economic times prompted many disputes by workers over the low wages offered by the factories. As a result, many workers went on strike to obtain higher salaries.

Much of the negativity surrounding the disputes was forgotten for a time in 1893 when the Columbian Exposition, the first great World's Fair for the city, opened to celebrate the 400th anniversary of Christopher Columbus's voyage to America. Bringing twenty-seven million visitors, a number nearly half the population of the United States at that time, the fair introduced Chicago as a forerunner in architectural greatness and technological initiative. In the downtown Chicago of the 1890s, typewriters and elevators were taking their rightful places in the dawn of a new type of building—the skyscraper—which gave Chicago its nickname, "the City of Big Shoulders." Proud Chicagoans boasted to the world of their great Exposition, and so earned their city the nickname, "the Windy City" because of the supposed hot air that came out of their mouths! Still, Chicago maintains its descriptive name as the tall skyscrapers force strong winds through the city.

In the twentieth century, hard economic times came and resulted in decay in some parts of the city. Then in the 1920s, the United States Congress passed the Prohibition law, which made alcohol illegal, and corruption and organized crime arrived in Chicago. Due to the illegality of alcohol, some people ventured into bootlegging, the selling of alcohol illegally, and became rich. Johnny Torrio was the first big boss of the Chicago crime family, but Torrio was soon sent back to Italy by the young and infamous Al Capone, who became the most powerful man in Chicago. On February 14, 1929, he reportedly had his men execute seven of his enemies in what has become known as the Valentine's Day Massacre.

At the end of the 1920s and in the early 1930s, Chicago was hit hard by the Great Depression. In 1933 and 1934, Chicago hosted another successful World's Fair, the Century of Progress Exposition, which displayed incredible futuristic exhibits. Although the fair helped to raise the spirits of the city, its presence contrasted sharply with the reality of the Great Depression.

After the Great Depression, blues music debuted in Chicago, revolutionized by the legendary Muddy Waters, who had moved north from Mississippi in 1943. The distinctive sound of Chicago blues has had a profound influence on all music in the second half of the twentieth century.

Today Chicago is known for its many blues clubs, but it is also known for its beautiful architecture, great shopping on Michigan Avenue's magnificent mile and its tasty deep dish pizza. Many of the buildings built as a result of the Great Fire still stand. Others built over the years, like the second tallest in the world, the Sears Tower, have become famous landmarks. The city is also home to one of the best museums in the United States, the Art Institute of Chicago, which houses a diverse collection valued at over $250 million dollars.

All of this wealth in history, architecture, music, and art has attracted a diverse immigrant population to the city. It is home to people from many countries and regions, such as Haiti, Latin America, the Middle East, Southeast Asia, and the former Soviet Union. Although there have been problems between ethnic groups in the past, Chicago is today promoting harmony among its people and is a welcoming city to visitors from near and far.

Boston, Massachusetts

Along the coast of the Atlantic Ocean in eastern Massachusetts is Boston, one of the oldest cities in the United States. Boston has a rich tradition in history, patriotism, and education and is still home to beautiful colonial structures, well known political leaders, and some of the finest universities in the nation.

The English Puritans, who founded the city in 1630, named it after the town of Boston, England, where many of them had lived. The Shawmut Peninsula, on which Boston is located, was first settled by the Shawmut tribe of Native Americans. However, by the time the Puritans arrived in the New World, most of the Native Americans had been killed by European diseases introduced by earlier settlers. In 1632, Boston became the capital of the Massachusetts Bay Colony, which included Boston, Plymouth to the south, and Salem to the north.

The Puritans had left England because they had been punished for expressing their religious beliefs. Ironically, the town leaders tried to punish anyone who did not share their same Puritan ideas. The Puritan settlers formed a close and extremely religious community, but still supported strict laws— for most infractions. They considered cooking on Sunday, the Sabbath day, a sin, so many Puritan women prepared baked beans every Saturday night and served them for Sunday dinner, which is what earned Boston the nickname "Beantown." In spite of its puritanical beginnings, by 1720, Boston had become a thriving town, with a population of twelve thousand people from various political and religious backgrounds. By the middle of the eighteenth century, Boston was a leading commercial center in the British colonies of America. Wealthy merchants became town leaders, and most of the strict laws enacted by the Puritans were forgotten.

In 1765, the colonies in America were in conflict with Great Britain, so colonists in Boston acted as the leaders in the struggle for independence. In 1770, some angry citizens of Boston turned against British soldiers when a street fight erupted in downtown Boston. The soldiers fired their muskets into the mob, killing five men and wounding six others. This incident became known as the Boston Massacre, a famous event that led to the beginning of the American Revolution. In 1773, a group of angry colonists called the Sons of Liberty dressed as Native Americans and planned what has become known as the Boston Tea Party in order to protest an unfair British tax on imported tea. The Sons of Liberty sneaked onto British ships in Boston Harbor and dumped the cargoes of tea into the water. This incident lead to three major battles of the American Revolution—the battles at Lexington, Concord, and Bunker Hill—which were fought near Boston in 1775. Then in March 1776, General George Washington and his troops forced the occupying British out of Boston, securing the first major American victory of the Revolution and eventually leading to American independence.

The nineteenth century was a period of huge growth for the city. Wealthy Boston merchants successfully entered into foreign trade. Ships loaded with local products like fish, rum, salt, and tobacco left for ports all over the world. The same ships returned with silk and tea from China, sugar and molasses from the West Indies, and gold and mahogany from Africa.

Between 1822 and 1858, many landfill projects more than doubled the physical size of the city. The extra space was much needed, as more than 500,000 Irish immigrants, fleeing the potato famine, had arrived in Boston during the 1840s. The immigrants, who could only afford to live in the crowded slums of the city, provided cheap labor for the factories and warehouses. Hostility arose among native Bostonians who did not trust the Irish, prompting some of these Bostonians to put signs in the windows of their businesses that said, "No Irish Need Apply," preventing many Irish from holding good jobs.

In November 1872, a fire broke out in downtown Boston that destroyed much of the city. The area was soon rebuilt, and the city continued to grow. Progress continued, and in 1897, the nation's first subway system opened in the city. By 1900, the population of Boston had grown to five hundred thousand.

By the end of the 1800s, the descendants of the Irish immigrants began to dominate the political scene. John J. Fitzgerald, the grandfather of President John F. Kennedy, served five years as the city's mayor. James M. Curley, a powerful rival to Fitzgerald, was elected four times as mayor of Boston between 1914 and 1950. Both men gave many jobs to their Irish supporters, helping to increase the economic and political power of the Irish in Boston, which still exists today.

Today, Boston is a beautiful city in which historic buildings are found alongside modern ones. The sights of Boston attract millions of visitors each year. The city's famous Freedom Trail, a one-and-a-half mile red path, allows visitors to roam the city on foot, bringing them to most of the historic spots in the downtown area, including Fanueil Hall, a meeting hall where the Sons of Liberty met to plan their moves against the British during the American Revolution; the site of the Boston Massacre; the Old North Church, where Paul Revere signaled the coming of the British during the Revolution by hanging two lanterns in the belfry; and the Old South Meeting House, where the Sons of Liberty met before the Boston Tea Party. The Boston Common, the nation's oldest public park, is the start of the Freedom Trail. The land for the Common was set aside by John Winthrop, the leader of the Puritans, to serve as a military training field and public cow pasture. Today the Common is a popular place for people to walk and rest in downtown Boston.

The city has long been a center of culture and education in the United States. The Boston Symphony Orchestra and the Boston "Pops" Orchestra provide wonderful music to Bostonians at Symphony Hall. The city is also graced by many wonderful museums, including the Museum of Fine Arts, which houses a collection representing nearly every culture of the last five thousand years. Nearby is the Isabella Stewart Gardner Museum, home to a once private collection of Renaissance paintings and sculptures, housed in a beautifully furnished Italian-style villa. Boston also has more than twenty colleges and universities, such as Boston University, Northeastern University, the University of Massachusetts—Boston, and Boston College, with Harvard University and the Massachusetts Institute of Technology located across the river in Cambridge.

Boston is a city full of history, culture, and beauty. It has helped greatly to shape the cultural and political history of the United States and is a wonderful place to start a historical tour of the country.

New York, New York

With a population of about seven and a half million, New York City is the largest city in the United States. The city is made up of five boroughs, or areas, which include the Bronx, Brooklyn, Manhattan, Queens, and Staten Island. Above all, New York is an international city for finance, business, and communications. Located on the East Coast of the United States between Long Island Sound and the Hudson River, New York is famous for its history, culture, and towering skyline.

This natural site for a great metropolitan area, where two rivers and a protected harbor converge, was first discovered in 1524 by Giovanni da Verrazano, an Italian explorer working for France. At that time, what became New York City was the home of the Canarsee, Manhattan, and Rockaway Native American tribes. Despite Verrazano's discovery, no European settlement was made until 1609, when the Dutch East India Company hired Englishman Henry Hudson to travel to the area. On September 3 of that year, Hudson sailed his boat up the river that was later named after him. The Dutch company made many more expeditions to the area over the next ten years, leading to the establishment of the first permanent settlement in 1626 in the area they called New Amsterdam. In that year a boat full of one hundred Protestant men, women, and children arrived in the new settlement. Because the government of New Amsterdam was tolerant of religious freedom and of different immigrant populations, people from all over Europe decided to settle there. As a result, by 1643, eighteen different languages were spoken in the growing town.

In 1625, the newly named Dutch West India Company sent Peter Minuit to New Amsterdam to hold the office of director general of New Netherlands, the area around New York that included New

Amsterdam. To make peace with the Native Americans, Minuit purchased the island of Manhattan from the Carnarsees for a number of small tools and trinkets. Relations between the Native Americans and the Dutch were friendly at first, but problems began when the Dutch moved closer and closer to Native American settlements. The worst of the conflicts came in 1641, when the Dutch decided to tax the Native Americans to help pay for the Dutch fort. The Native Americans refused to pay. The Dutch retaliated by attacking the Native Americans without warning in February 1643. This led to a war with the Native Americans that lasted more than two years. After the Native Americans surrendered, there were no more major disturbances between the two groups in New Amsterdam.

The British, who controlled the other colonies on the East Coast of the United States, saw the Dutch presence in New Amsterdam as a nuisance. In 1664, the British sailed to New York and took control of New Amsterdam without any resistance from the Dutch. To honor the Duke of York, the British quickly changed the name of the settlement to New York. Under British colonial rule, New York exchanged agricultural products for manufactured goods from Britain, rum and coffee from the West Indies, and slaves from Africa.

By the time of the American Revolution in 1776, New York had become an established commercial center. At first, the American settlers in New York revolted against British rule. They destroyed a metal statue of King George III, melting it down to make bullets. However, only months later, the British took control of New York for the rest of the war. The British decided to make New York their headquarters in North America because it was centrally located between Massachusetts and Virginia, the other two most important colonies at that time. Many people loyal to the British government immigrated to New York from other colonies. Businesses prospered because the British army brought lots of money to the local economy. When the American Revolution finally came to an end in 1783 with an American victory, the last British troops were forced to leave New York City.

In 1789, New York was chosen to be the first capital of the United States of America. The inauguration of General George Washington as the first president took place on the balcony of Federal Hall. Although New York lost its status as the nation's capital to Philadelphia only one year later, it was by then the largest city in the new country. The city was also considered the unofficial trading and financial capital of the United States.

Through the port of New York came products from all over the world. With the opening of the Erie Canal in upstate New York in 1825, the city played a major role in distributing products to the interior parts of the United States. Beginning in the 1840s, New York's role as a world city began to attract millions of immigrants from Europe. Between 1880 and 1919, more than seventeen million immigrants arrived in New York through the immigration center at Ellis Island in New York Harbor. They caught their first glimpse of the promise of a better life as they sailed past the Statue of Liberty, a gift given to the United States by France in 1876 in recognition of 100 years of independence. No one knows how many of these immigrants actually stayed in the city, but as early as 1840, more than half of the local working population was foreign born. Visitors could walk for miles in New York without ever hearing the English language.

In the 1870s, the African American population of New York was very small, but it started to rise again in the 1880s when African Americans moved in from the southern United States. The largest concentration of African Americans was found in Harlem, to which African Americans began to move in 1905. Although technically still part of New York City, by 1930 Harlem was widely known as the largest "black city" in the world. In fact, it was the Harlem jazz musicians who dubbed New York City "the Big Apple" in the early twentieth century.

Since 1924, Puerto Ricans and other Hispanics, along with African Americans moving up from the South, have added to the large population growth within the city limits. As late as 1980, approximately one out of every four New Yorkers had been born outside of the United States. The city is said to have one of the largest Jewish communities in the world and possibly the largest Italian population outside of Italy. Today, eighty percent of the population of New York City is made up of five ethnic groups: African American, Irish, Italian, Jewish, and Puerto Rican.

Although the African American and Hispanic populations of New York increased between 1970 and 1980, the overall population of the city declined. Those who remained were either very rich or very poor. Most of the rich live in Manhattan, near the centers of business and culture. Still, nearly fifteen percent of all families in New York live in poverty. With so many living so poorly, New York's vitality has been affected by such problems as illiteracy, drug abuse, racism, and homelessness.

Nevertheless, New York City thrives due to the presence of some of the best cultural institutions in the nation, including the Metropolitan Museum of Art, which contains more than two thousand European paintings, three thousand American paintings, and the entire Egyptian temple of Dendur. Classical music is also very prominent in New York City. Carnegie Hall is one of the world's great music halls where many musicians dream of playing. Broadway is home to some of the best theater performances in the United States, rivaling London as the premiere theater city in the world. Evening entertainment is also provided by thousands of restaurants, clubs, and bars, most of which are open all night, earning the city the nickname "the City that Never Sleeps." New York has become the center for nearly everything in the United States, from the arts to finance and from fashion to communications. It is truly one American city that should not be missed.

Photography Credits

Phoenix, Arizona
Phoenix skyline, courtesy of Digital Stock Corporation, page 1
Mission building, courtesy of Michael Quan, page 6

Vancouver, British Columbia
Vancouver skyline, courtesy of Digital Stock Corporation, page 13
Lion's Gate Bridge, © The Learning Company, Inc. and its licensors, page 17

Philadelphia, Pennsylvania
Philadelphia skyline, courtesy of Digital Stock Corporation, page 25
Statue of George Washington in front of Independence Hall, courtesy of Mike Bell, page 28
Liberty Bell, courtesy of Mike Bell, page 30
Mural of "Boy," courtesy of Mike Bell, page 37

Honolulu, Hawaii
Honolulu skyline, courtesy of Digital Stock Corporation, page 42
Waikiki Beach, courtesy of Michael Quan, page 46
Side Trip: Hawaii Volcanoes National Park
Lava hitting the ocean, courtesy of Michael Quan, page 53
Truck in lava, courtesy of Michael Quan, page 54

Los Angeles, California
Los Angeles skyline, courtesy of Digital Stock Corporation, page 55
On the set of a TV program, courtesy of the author, page 58
J. Paul Getty Museum, courtesy of the author, page 64

Miami, Florida
Miami skyline, courtesy of Digital Stock Corporation, page 67
Colony Hotel, courtesy of Michael Quan, page 71
People on Miami Beach, courtesy of Judi Kadden, page 76

Las Vegas, Nevada
Las Vegas lights, courtesy of Digital Stock Corporation, page 78
Las Vegas skyline, courtesy of Digital Stock Corporation, page 87
Hoover Dam, courtesy of Judi Kadden, page 91
Side Trip: The Grand Canyon
Views of Grand Canyon, courtesy of Mike Bell, pages 93, 94

Montréal, Québec
Montréal skyline, courtesy of Digital Stock Corporation, page 95
Political graffiti, courtesy of the author, page 99
Montréal street scene, courtesy of the author, page 103

Washington, D.C.
Crowd on steps of Capitol, courtesy of Digital Stock Corporation, page 107
Nighttime view of the Capitol, courtesy of Digital Stock Corporation, page 111

Views of the monuments, courtesy of Digital Stock Corporation, page 118

Side Trip: Colonial Williamsburg, Virginia

Horse drawn carriage in front of house, courtesy of Mike Bell, page 120

A street scene in Colonial Williamsburg, courtesy of Mike Bell, page 121

Chicago, Illinois

Chicago skyline, courtesy of Digital Stock Corporation, page **122**

Chicago River, courtesy of Michael Quan, page 124

Lake Michigan beach scene, courtesy of Michael Quan, page 127

Ruins after the Great Chicago Fire, from the Nov. 4, 1871 issue of *Harper's Weekly,* page 130

The Sears Tower, courtesy of Michael Quan, page 135

Boston, Massachusetts

Charles River and Hancock Tower, courtesy of Michael Quan, page 138

Swan boats in Boston Public Garden, courtesy of Michael Quan, page 142

View of Fanueil Hall, courtesy of Digital Stock Corporation, page **151**

New York, New York

Boat crossing Manhattan skyline, courtesy of Michael Quan, page 153

Empire State Building, courtesy of Digital Stock Corporation, page 157

Central Park, courtesy of Digital Stock Corporation, page 166

Text Credits

Phoenix, Arizona

"Hohokam Pottery Turning to Dust on Museum Shelves; Humidity Fluctuations Leave Artifacts 'Vulnerable,'" from the *Arizona Republic,* February 20, 1995, by Miriam Davidson. Copyright 1995, Phoenix Newspapers Inc. Reprinted with permission.

Vancouver, British Columbia

"Not China, but Close: Vancouver Is the Closest Thing to an Asian Bargain," from *USA Today,* August 11, 1995, by Barbranda Lumpkins. Copyright 1995, USA Today. Reprinted with permission.

Philadelphia, Pennsylvania

"A Mural Program to Turn Graffiti Offenders Around," from *Smithsonian Magazine,* July 1993, by Steven Barboza. Reprinted with the permission of Steven Barboza.

Honolulu, Hawaii

"Hawaii Families Resettle on Land," from *Associated Press,* March 16, 1997, by Meki Cox. Copyright 1997, Associated Press. Reprinted with permission.

Los Angeles, California

"A Rags-to-Riches Tale Right out of Hollywood; Miramax Deal Means Big Bucks for Bartender," from *USA Today,* April 16, 1997, by Elizabeth Snead. Copyright 1997, USA Today. Reprinted with permission.